Investing in Property with Str

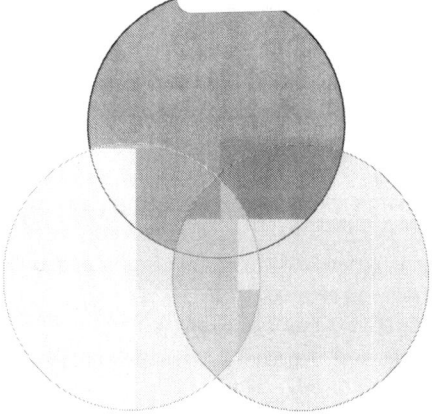

Quantum Technique: A Winning Formula for Wealth Creation.

Godwin Okri

Published by New Generation Publishing in 2015

Copyright © Godwin Okri 2015

First Edition

The author asserts the moral right under the Copyright, Designs and Patents Act 1988 to be identified as the author of this work.

All Rights reserved. No part of this publication may be reproduced, stored in a retrieval system or transmitted, in any form or by any means without the prior consent of the author, nor be otherwise circulated in any form of binding or cover other than that which it is published and without a similar condition being imposed on the subsequent purchaser.

www.newgeneration-publishing.com

 New Generation Publishing

CONTENTS

About the author i
INTRODUCTION 1
CHAPTER 1: Quantum Theory and Property Investments 3
CHAPTER 2: The Science of Property Investments . 6
CHAPTER 3: Why Invest in Property 19
CHAPTER 4: Where to Invest 24
CHAPTER 5: When to Invest 33
CHAPTER 6: What to Invest In 42
CHAPTER 7: How to Invest/Raising Funds 49
CHAPTER 8: Purchasing With No Money Down ... 66
CHAPTER 9: The Mathematics of Property Investments 74
CHAPTER 10: The Mathematics of Stamp Duty .. 100
CHAPTER 11: The Economics of Property Investments 102
APPENDICES 109
APPENDIX i: The Pareto Principle 110
APPENDIX ii: How to Find Property Bargains 111
APPENDIX iii: Step-by-step Property Transaction Guide 113
POSTSCRIPT: Unencumbered Property: A Better Derivative 121

About the author

Godwin Okri is an employed Barrister (non-practising) and CEO at Menvo Limited, a property investment company. He is also a seasoned real estate investor with 13 years' experience since 2002.

He has presented numerous property seminars in the UK, USA and Africa, with over 4,000 people attending his seminar in 2009 alone.

Mr Okri's groundbreaking book highlights the application of cutting-edge science in property investments.

He lives in Kent and has four children. His daughter was a semi-finalist at the 2008 Britain's Got Talent competition.

INTRODUCTION
"The universe began as a story" – Ben Okri

The field of real estate is vast; it is an interesting aspect of humanity.

I am aware that there are many books written on this subject, particularly from an economic perspective. The global recession, which started in 2008, made this subject a topical issue in social gatherings, parties and even at football matches! However, I believe that the reader would also find it helpful to see real estate investment from the viewpoint of science.

When I first started writing this book, I thought of giving it the title *The Science of Property Investment*, but I found that this was going to take away what I was trying to convey, which is this: if you invest in below-market-value (atomic) property in a strategic area and you add value (by improving that property), you can increase your energy of profit by repeating the same process (method). You can then cash in on your investment, the proceeds of which cumulatively could propel you to the high-value property market in places such as New York, London or Tokyo. The concept which best describes this is the quantum theory.

I have successfully applied this concept as a property investor since 2002. Also, as a legal and property consultant, I have observed some of my investor-clients successfully apply this concept. Further, I have presented numerous seminars in the UK and overseas (including the USA and Nigeria). Each time I speak to some of the attendees after the presentation, I noticed that a small number of them had also unknowingly applied this concept in their investments.

The aim of this book is to help the reader understand the basic principles of making money in property investments. Another purpose here is to introduce my readers to another way of thinking when investing in real estate.

I try to apply the quantum theory in real estate investment in a very simplistic way so that this can easily be applied by any investor of some intelligence. I do not expect my readers to be Albert Einstein or Stephen Hawkins. I have avoided trying to engage my readers at a deeper level. Instead, I have kept things simple and easy to understand. In fact, there is nothing in this book that the reader cannot understand so far as s/he has a reasonable level of education.

I am aware that not all my readers have a lot of time on their hands. For this reason, I try to make each chapter short and simple.

Towards the end of the book, there are several appendices to cover general topics that some investors may find useful and helpful.

Finally, remember the famous words of Ben Okri in his book *A Time For New Dreams*: 'Books are like mirrors. Don't just read the words. Go into the mirror. That is where the real secrets are. Inside. Behind. That's where the gods dream, where our realities are born.'

CHAPTER 1: QUANTUM THEORY AND PROPERTY INVESTMENTS

'You find greatness when you have maximised smallness' –
Unknown

Introduction

At first sight, the quantum theory may appear incompatible with property investing. However, if you look closely, you would find that quantum theory is at the heart of property investment.

The Theory

The theoretical basis of modern physics is undeniably the quantum theory; this theory explains the nature and behaviour of matter and energy on the atomic and subatomic level. One famous scientist, who is a quantum theorist, is Albert Einstein. His famous formula, $E = mc^2$ shows that the small mass can reflect massive energy. In other words, a body's mass can be considered a direct measure of the energy contained therein and vice versa.

The earlier scientists assumed that the physical state of a system could be measured exactly and used to predict future states. Thus, quantum theorists measure the smallest unit of something to determine its combined potency.

Practical Application

Quantum theory has universal applicability. This theory has even been applied in the field of economics: the 'quantity theory of money' is a key concept advocated by monetarists. The 'quantum of money' deals with the lowest-value coin in circulation. The monetarist says that a change in the lowest value of currency could change the general price level of an economy.

The savvy investor, engaged in real estate investment, can also adopt and utilise the philosophy contained in the quantum theory.

The philosophy contained within the quantum theory, when applied to property investment, is this: if you invest in below-market-value (atomic) property in a strategic area and you add value (by improving that property), you can increase your energy of profit by repeating the same process (method). Thus, by increasing the portfolio of acquired properties in this way would eventually increase your energy of profit.

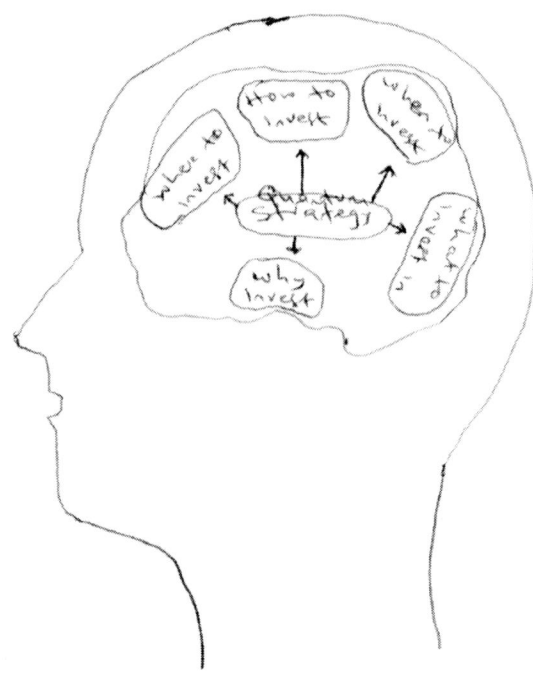

In order to generate the energy of profit required when investing in property, the following are important:

Firstly, you must mentally assess why you want to invest in real estate. (See *Why Invest in Properties* in chapter 3).

Secondly, you must invest in an up and coming area, where demand is about to take off. (See *Where to Invest* in chapter 4).

Thirdly, you must assess the property market and determine when to invest. (See *When to Invest* in chapter 5).

Fourthly, you must choose what type of asset to invest in. (See *What to Invest In*, in chapter 6).

Lastly, you must work out ways to raise funds for your property investments. (See *How to Invest/Raising Funds* in chapter 7).

CHAPTER 2: THE SCIENCE OF PROPERTY INVESTMENTS

Physics have long been the preserve of scientists, until now.

INTRODUCTION

To be a successful property investor, you need to have a workable formula, which, if applied, would yield positive results. In this chapter, I want to demonstrate how a property investor can apply the quantum theory to generate wealth and achieve financial independence.

PROPERTY QUANTUM FORMULA

Having studied the quantum theory, and having successfully applied it since 2002 as an investor, I believe I have found the formula which a property investor can apply when investing in property. The formula is known as the 'Property Quantum Formula' (PQF). The mathematical equation of my formula is $\mathbf{E = MXV}$. This equation, when applied to real estate investment, appears to be an epexegesis of Einstein's $E = mc^2$.

The acronym $\mathbf{E = MXV}$ is this:

'E' stands for 'energy' of profit. This is the eventual profit an investor makes in a transaction (or a series of transactions).

'M' stands for 'mass'. In physics, 'mass' describes the amount of matter in an object. Here, 'mass' refers to each low-value property. These are properties bought below market value (BMV). I also refer to them as 'atomic' or 'quantum' properties.

'X' stands for any chosen number of properties an investor has budgeted to buy over a certain period of time. An investor is free to choose how many properties he wishes to buy and sell/rent out in a specified period of time. Each investor's capacity or appetite for investment is different. Thus, 'X' takes account of the idiosyncrasy of the individual investor.

'V' stands for 'velocity'. The speed a property is bought, improved and sold/rented is referred to as 'velocity'. It also means the speed of purchase. 'Velocity' is enhanced by being able to raised fund by 'leveraging'. See 'leverage' below.

The sum total of this formula is this: the 'energy' of profit capable of being generated in an investment is a function of the number of below market value properties bought, improved and sold/rented out at certain speed or regularity.

Put another way, the profit a person may make when investing in property will depend on him acquiring 'bargain' property which is then reasonably improved and sold on or rented out. However, it is the speed or regularity at which this is done that guarantee an investor's level of profit. The scenario in example 3 below illustrates the effectiveness of PQF as a strategy to generate wealth in the property market.

In addition, the above formula also teaches an investor to be methodical when investing in property.

Consider this example:

EXAMPLE 1

Joe is planning to acquire 3 bargain properties in Leeds within 1 year. How can this be achieved using the Property Quantum Formula (PQF)?

We need to apply **PQF**'s mathematical equation, which is: $E = MXV$.

Since we know the number of bargain properties Joe wants, we now know that 'X' equals 3 bargain properties. The speed (i.e. 'velocity') at which these properties are to be purchased is that the 3 bargain properties must be purchased within the time limit of 12 months.

This can now be expressed as:

   $3X$ = **12V** (i.e. 3 properties ('X') to the acquired within 12 months 'V')

So, X = **4V** (which means that Joe must endeavour to acquire at least 1 property every 4 months)

Or, $.5X$ = **2V** (which means that, every 2 months, Joe must have at least 50% of the cost of 1 property in his possession)

How to raise funds is covered in chapter 7.

In order to benefit from the **PQF**, the following are important:

 (a) Leverage;
 (b) Velocity; and
 (c) Value Engineering.

a) LEVERAGE

To some, the word 'leverage' has scientific origin. In science, leverage is a mechanical advantage gained by using a tool called a lever. A lever is a simple machine consisting of a bar that pivots on a fixed support, or fulcrum, and is used to lift a load. A force applied by pushing down on one end of the lever results in a force pushing up at the other end.

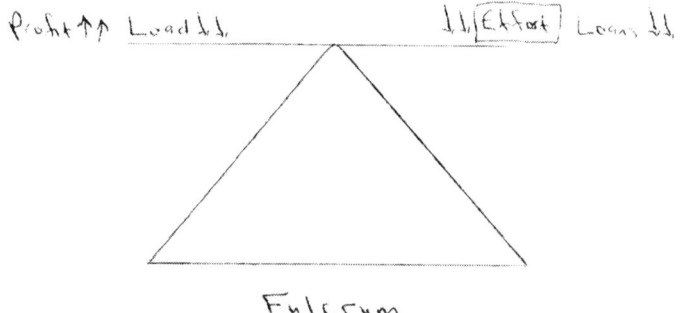

In the field of business and economics (to which property investment is a part), leverage takes a similar meaning. It refers to using borrowed money to increase the potential return of an investment and, as a result, earnings. That is, using other people's money to gain an investment advantage in the market. It is the ability to do more with less.

Consider this example:

EXAMPLE 2

James has £100,000 and wants to invest in property in an area where price increases by 7% yearly. If he uses his £100,000 to make an outright purchase, next year the property would be worth £107,000, giving him an increase of £7,000.

Alternatively, James may decide to leverage so as to be able to purchase a property for £400,000. He puts down his £100,000 as a deposit and takes out a mortgage for £300,000. In a year the house would be worth £428,000, an increase of £28,000. James, through using the lender's money as leverage, has made 4 times the amount than he would have made without leveraging.

In this example, 25% down payment gets James 100% of the house. He has achieved more with less.

Obtaining a buy-to-let (BTL) mortgage is an excellent way to leverage. There are also other ways funds can be raised. I covered this in chapter 7. Having funds will clearly give you an advantage as this will facilitate your access into the property investment market.

(b) VELOCITY

In physics, velocity is a measurement of the speed of an object. The most common way to calculate the constant velocity of an object moving in a straight line is with the formula:

$$R = \frac{D}{T}$$

In order words: Speed = $\frac{\text{Distance}}{\text{Time}}$

Scientists prefer to think about speed in metres and seconds, since metres and seconds are basic SI units whose small size gives more accurate result. So, the speed of sound is roughly 340 meters per second and the speed of light is about 300,000,000 meters per second.

When it comes to investment, velocity is the speed (or 'rate') at which your initial investment is used or employed to generate greater returns. An investor who buys 3 bargain properties with 1 year has a faster velocity than an investor who merely buys 1 property within a 12 month period.

Consider this example:

EXAMPLE 3

James has £100,000 and wants to invest it for 3 years in a property market where price increases at the rate of 7% per year.

The first approach is this:

If he buys 1 property outright for £100,000, then at the end of the third year he would earn extra £22,504.30, if he were to sell.

This is illustrated below:

Year	Previous Value	7% Increase	Profit
Year 1	£100,000	£107,000	£7,000
Year 2	£107,000	£114,490	£7,490
Year 3	£114,490	£122,504.30	£8,014.30
			£22,504.30

The alternative approach is this:

Instead of buying 1 property, James decides to apply the 'Property Quantum Formula'. If this formula is applied, the outcome could be as follows:

Year 1

Applying velocity, James buys 3 properties at the price of £100,000 each. He puts down £30,000 of his own money on each property and obtains a mortgage of £70,000 for the balance on each property. This is illustrated below:

Property	Price	Deposit	Loan
Property 1	£100,000	£30,000	£70,000
Property 2	£100,000	£30,000	£70,000
Property 3	£100,000	£30,000	£70,000

Year 2

James, intending to increase the velocity of his investments, decides to re-mortgage the 3 properties so as to raise extra cash to buy additional property.

In order to re-mortgage, James applies to another bank for a new mortgage. The new bank values each property for £107,000 (i.e. 7% increase in price) and agrees to lend James £74,900 for each property. James takes the loan and pays off (i.e. redeems) the old mortgage of £70,000 per property and retains the excess amount of £4,900 per property. James can now raise £4,900 x 3 = £14,700.

The illustration below shows the calculation:

Property	New Loan Raised	Pay off old Loan	Excess Amount Retained
Property 1	£74,900	£70,000	£4,900
Property 2	£74,900	£70,000	£4,900
Property 3	£74,900	£70,000	£4,900
			£14,700

In the same year, James buys another property (i.e. property 4) for the price of £107,000, using the extra £14,900 as a down payment and taking out another mortgage of £92,100 for the balance.

Year 3

James sells all his properties for the price of £114,490 each, since they have increased in value by a further 7%. This can be illustrated as follows:

Property	Sale Price	Amount needed to repay the Loan	Profit
Property 1	£114,490	£74,900	£39,540
Property 2	£114,490	£74,900	£39,540
Property 3	£114,490	£74,900	£39,540
Property 4	£114,490	£92,100	£22,390
			£141,010

From the illustrations above, you can see that the 'energy' of profit generated when James bought 1 property outright was £22,504.30.

However, the 'energy' of his profit increased substantially to £141,010 when he increased the speed of his investment (buying 4 properties), which was made possible by using the lender's money (i.e. leveraging).

In order to achieve the desired level of profit, you need to show mental fortitude. If you are fully determined by setting out a realistic goal as to the number of bargain properties you wish to acquire, and working out your source of funds (see chapter 7), then you would be well on your way to increasing your assets and, eventually, wealth.

(c) VALUE ENGINEERING

Value engineering is an aspect of science that involves systematic method of improving the 'value' of something by enhancing its functions at reasonable costs.

The idea about value engineering began at General Electric Co. during World War II, when there was a chronic shortage of parts and acceptable substitutes had to be used at reduced costs.

In property investment, applying value engineering is important. *For the investor, value engineering involves repairing, renovating and maintaining a property with a view to increasing its value.*

Put simply, if you invest in below market value (atomic) property in a strategic area and you add value, using value engineering, you can increase your 'energy' of profit by repeating the same process (method). This would eventually enable you invest in the high value property market such as London, New York or Cape Town.

When enhancing 'value', it is important not to over improve the property.
 An 'over improvement' occurs when an investor invests more money in renovation than he can reasonably expect to recoup.

Consider this example:

EXAMPLE 4

James owns a 2 bed property in an area where the average price of a 2 bed house is £150,000. He decides to spend £35,000 to build a swimming pool. This increased the value of his house to £160,000. Since he cannot recoup the extra £25,000 spent on the property, this would be an 'over improvement', and would go against the value engineering concept.

Another important factor to consider here is what a property's 'highest and best use' is. The most profitable use to which a property may be put is that property's 'highest and best use'.

Consider this example:

EXAMPLE 5

Assuming James is deciding whether to spend £10,000 to convert a property into a 1 bed flat resulting in a rental income of £450 per month or spend £12,000 converting the same property into a 2 bed flat with rental income of £700 per month. Which is the property's highest and best use?

The 'highest and best use' would be to convert the property into a 2 bed flat. By spending an extra £2,000 (taking your total expenditure to £12,000), you get an extra bedroom, which earns you £3,000 more in rent per year.

The illustration below shows the calculation:

Type of Flat	Cost of Conversion	Annual Rent Yield	Highest & Best return
1 Bed	£10,000	£5,400	Nil
2 Bed	£12,000	£8,400	£3,000 extra

Further, it is important to use competent contractors (such as builders, plumbers, electricians, architects, etc.) when enhancing the 'value' of your property. Rarely will you find a BMV bargain property in perfect condition. More often than not, you will need to carry out some repairs or renovation. Older properties tend to require more repairs than newer properties. Cosmetic repairs do not require special knowledge. However, major repairs require experienced contractors. You, therefore, would need to build your own team of contractors, not least, because they can offer you support and expertise in their field of specialization.

You can find contractors from various sources:

- Adverts in a local paper
- Contractors on the list of the local estate agent
- Recommendations from family and friends
- Google, Thompson Directory, Yellow Pages, etc.

When selecting your team of contractors, you may ask for the following:

- Details, photographs and/or videos of the most recent projects by the contractors
- References
- Type of projects they have worked on
- The time it has taken to complete various tasks
- Details about fees and costs of material (if relevant)
- What their system of work is. Do they outsource?
- Do they have insurance?
- Are they regulated by an authorised body or trade organisation?

When instructing your team of contractors to undertake renovation work, they must consider whether planning permission is required for that work. If so, the necessary application must be made.

There are some building extensions for which planning permission is not required if undertaking under Permitted

Development. If you are not sure, check with the Planning Department of the local authority concerned.

Even if planning permission is not required for the repairs or renovation, you may still be required to obtain Building Regulations approval from the relevant local authority. Building Regulations approval would be required if you are installing new windows or installing cavity insulation or relocating the kitchen/bathroom or removing the load-bearing walls in the building, etc. After the work has been completed to the satisfaction of the Council, then a Building Regulations Approval Certificate would be issued to the owner. You may not be able to sell your property without this certificate, if an approval is required.

Finally, when enhancing the 'value' of your property, the following are important:

(i) Kitchen: The kitchen is an important area. Most tenants or buyers are influenced by the state of the kitchen. So, if the kitchen units are dated and the appliances are not clean or fresh, replace them. You can buy fairly new units and appliances for a reasonable price. A tiled kitchen floor would also create a good impression.

(ii) Bathroom: The bathroom is another area that can impress or put off a tenant or buyer. Thus, if the bath is in a poor condition or not white, change it. Also, tile the floor and wall with white or bright colour. If the toilet and seat are outdated and cannot be cleaned, replace them. Ensure that the bath, toilet and washbasin are in the same colour, preferably white. A fresh bathroom creates a long lasting impression.

(iii) Other parts of the property: The value of a property can be increased, firstly, by improving the internal layout of that property. Tenants and buyers prefer properties with upstairs bathrooms and sizeable bedrooms. Thus, relocating the bathroom upstairs and the kitchen downstairs would add value. The layout of the property should be user-friendly.

Value can also be increased by putting in gas central heating (if required), updating the electrics, painting the whole house and either installing carpets in the whole rooms or laminating the floors.

(iv) Outside: The external appearance of any property affects its curb appeal. Thus, a property's value can be enhanced by ensuring that the lawn is cut; the shrubs or trees are pruned; the windows are double-glazed (if the property is a flat, check with the landlord first); the roof is watertight; and the gutters and down-pipes are in good order.

In summary, the engineering of the value of a property through repairs and renovation effectively increases the monetary value of that investment property, which in turn increases the wealth of the investor.

CONCLUSION

It is folly to think that science is only confined to physics, chemistry and biology. Science is far more accessible than many scientists would have us believe. Most concepts and theories in science have universal applicability. *There is a science to everything.*

As shown above, science has extended its generous hands to the area of property investment. The PQF has scientific underpinning. So, by leveraging, by investing with repeated speed and by improving the investment property as you go along, you can increase your asset and, thereby, create wealth.

CHAPTER 3: WHY INVEST IN PROPERTY

'In small numbers comes big outcome' – G.O

Investing in 'bricks and mortar' is now a popular investment habit in the whole world. At parties, social gatherings and the like, the most common subject of discussion is often the property market.

If you look all around you, you will see that people are beginning to appreciate the benefits of property investments. In fact, in late 2014, Enfield Council broke with tradition and went ahead to form a company with a view to investing in properties. In early 2015, Westminster Council began purchasing properties outside London because of shortage of properties. The limited housing stock caused by tenants buying up council flats is a contributory factor.

What then are the benefits of investing in properties? Why invest in properties?

(a) Wealth Creation

Most people invest in real estate to generate wealth. There are now almost 2 million buy-to-let landlords owning £1 trillion of property.

In early 2015, the English Housing Survey (which was commissioned by the Bank of England) showed that the proportion of households in England who owned their homes outright (without any mortgage) outstrip the proportion of households who own their homes with a mortgage. There were 7.4 million outright owners versus 6.9 million who own homes with a mortgage.

According to Lloyds TSB Private Banking, in 2012 housing wealth (i.e. the value of housing less outstanding mortgages) increased by £1 trillion over the last ten years. Housing wealth has grown faster than incomes. The value of the UK housing is now estimated at about £5.75 trillion. The housing stock in London is worth £1.5 trillion. The total value of housing across North West, North East and Yorkshire & the Humber rose by £42 billion over a decade. From these, it is understandable why we are obsessed with investing in bricks and mortar.

Apart from wealth creation generated from capital appreciation, investors would also benefit from 'cash flow' from rental income.

The rate of increase of house prices in the UK has prevented first-time buyers from being able to access the property ladder. The English Housing Survey showed that people aged between 25 and 34 were now more likely to be renting privately than buying. As a result, the overall average rents are rising in the UK. For instance, in 2015 there was a 7% increase in rent in Manchester. In England, buy-to-let landlords banked almost £4 billion a month in rental income in the first quarter of 2015.

(b) Pension

Another reason to invest in real estate is to create a pension plan so that when you retire, you have a guaranteed stream of regular income in the form of rents received from your property.

Prior to April 2015, the pension system in the UK had been ineffective. The large savings pot had become worth less and less. To compound matters, if you needed to draw down on your pension, tax was payable. The ineffectiveness of the whole system led the Conservative

Government to change the law. Now if you are over 55 years old, you are permitted to draw down some or all your pension and spend it as you see fit.

Some people buy annuity instead of property. An annuity is a kind of insurance product that ensures you receive a regular income for the rest of your life. It turns savings into regular monthly income.

I normally stay away from annuity because when you die your fund may go to the annuity provider. Some providers may offer guarantees that your next of kin would receive a lump sum, but after deduction of fees, etc they may not get anything like the money initially invested.

For this reason, I prefer investing in property. This will give you more autonomy and control over the management of your assets during your lifetime. You can also easily transfer its true nature in your will.

Property ownership works exactly like an annuity, only better. If you own it outright, you would have paid the initial purchase price at the outset. If it is mortgaged, you would pay your monthly premium to the mortgage company until it is fully paid. Your property (which is like a 'policy') would now earn you cash value. I see properties as long-term annuities.

(c.) Forced Saving Plan

One advantage of property investment is that after you have invested in it, your cash is tied up in this investment such that it prevents you from spending it recklessly. I know of some of my friends who have inadvertently become rich because once their money was stuck in the investment they could not quickly release it. So they hung on until the property increased in value.

Since properties that are rented gives return, investing in property is like putting your money in a savings account, only better. If you save £15,000 at the bank, the average interest you may get is 2% per annum. If you invest the same amount in a property in, say, Manchester as a deposit on a mortgage of £70,000. Your rent is likely to be £500 per month. Since interest rate is low, your mortgage should be no more than £350 per month. This would give you £150 per month, which is more than you would get in a savings account.

(d) Tax Shelter

Some economists have argued that investing in rental property creates a tax shield for income generated from the property. In England and Wales, the tax law allows buy-to-let investors certain tax relief, which effectively reduces their tax bill. These tax relief are known as 'allowable expenses'. There are numerous 'allowable expenses'. For instance, the tax law allows a buy-to-let investor to deduct from the rental income, amongst others, the cost of maintenance and repairs done to the investment property (but not for improvements) before paying tax on the net income.

The tax law also allows for tax relief on mortgage interest paid by the buy-to-let investor. This tax break allows landlords to deduct mortgage interest from their profits, thereby reducing their tax bill.

If the investment property is a furnished residential letting, the buy-to-let investor can also claim 10% of the net rent as 'wear and tear allowance'. Thus, property investment not only increases your asset worth, it also enables you to reduce your tax liability. Isn't that great!

(e) Inheritance

There are a number of people who invest in property with a view to leaving a suitable asset to their children when they die. This is sometimes referred to as inheritance.

   (i.) Will: It is important that you safeguard your investment property to ensure your children inherit it on your death. The best way to ensure your investment property is left to your children is by drawing up a will. It is best to seek legal advice before drawing up a will.
   (ii.) Intestacy: If a person dies without making a will, he is said to have died 'intestate'. The provisions of the Administration of Estates Act 1925, sets out who should benefit from your estate. For instance, where the deceased has a surviving spouse and children, the spouse would keep the personal chattels and the first £125,000. In relation to the investment property, the surviving spouse has a 'life interest'. However, title to the investment property would pass to the children when the surviving spouse eventually dies.

   Where you die leaving children with no surviving spouse, the children inherit the investment property equally.

Author's Remark

When I first started investing in properties, the issue of inheritance was not in my thought. I was initially interested in rental yields and capital appreciation. It was only recently that I began considering the importance of inheritance. I spoke with my wife about this, and we agreed that leaving something for our children would actually put them at an advantage in future.

CHAPTER 4: WHERE TO INVEST

Where to sow? "The small mustard seed is the foundation of faith" – G.O

When it comes to 'quantum property investment', location is an important factor to take into account. Where you invest is fundamental because you want to invest in an area with low-priced property but with good economic and employment prospects. This low-priced (atomic) property forms the basis of 'quantum investment' advocated in this book.

If you invest in low-priced (atomic) property in a strategic area and you add value (by improving the property), you can increase your 'energy' of profit by repeating the strategy. In other words, by adding each low-priced but improved property to your portfolio, you can eventually attain the cosmic value, which could facilitate entry into the high-value market such as London, New York, Cape Town, etc.

Every major city has high and low value areas. So, when determining the location to invest, look out for areas close to, but not inside, the high-value areas. There are a number of indicators to look out for, namely:

- (a) Business inflow and employment
- (b) Population growth
- (c) Public amenities and activities
- (d) Government's local policy
- (e) High yield
- (f) Capital appreciation

(a) Business Inflow and Employment

This is the most important indicator. Look out for areas where companies are moving in and jobs are being created. This is a sign that the area is on the up. It is important to note that people go where jobs are. In other words, population follows employment.

High employment can be beneficial for the up and coming area. It means you have a ready tenant who can afford to rent your property. It also means your 'quantum property', after improvement, would have a ready buyer who can afford to pay for the property.

It is important to look for trend; enter the local market early before it gets saturated and price starts to rise. If you invest in the area after price has risen, then your 'energy' of profit would be lost.

Almost all local authorities in England and Wales have a Business and Investments Unit, which provides socio-economic statistic about the area. This section of the local authority regularly publishes a range of local economic and performance data. This data are useful because they provide the investor with necessary material to gauge the level of business activities in the area.

(b) Population Growth

Another indicator of upward mobility is population growth. If you invest in an area where the population is growing, this creates a high pool of 'possible' tenants. In other words, increase in population would create a demand for properties to rent or buy.

People flock to areas where there are jobs. They also go to areas that are trendy, youthful and entertaining. I look for the following which draws in the population to an area: (a) new sports stadium and entertainment arenas; (b) universities, since they bring a steady stream of students; (c) improved transportation, which makes it accessible; (d) airports; (e) major events, such as concerts, carnivals, the Commonwealth Games, etc. All of these are major population drivers and are reliable indicators of growth.

If the area is touched by gentrification before you get there, then you may have arrived at the location a little late. You can still invest in the area. It just means that you simply have to search a little bit more thoroughly for the bargain 'quantum property'.

(c) Public Amenities and Activities

Areas where the public amenities are being improved are a good indicator that the location is up and coming. Look out for improved roads, rail or transportation. This brings the area closer to other high-value areas.

The redevelopment of an area and regeneration is a powerful indicator that the area is up and coming. People like to live in improved areas, which are accessible.

There are other indicators such as trendy wine bars, cafés, major high street banks, art galleries, fashion shops and new supermarkets opening. It is important to note that supermarkets such as Tesco, Morrison or Asda have entire departments dedicated to market research; they have in-depth research data on the demographics of an area.

Coffee shops such as Starbucks or Costa would have done market research about the area before opening up there.

Look out for developers such as Persimmons Homes, Bellway, etc. Where there are developers, this is a good sign. Developers have an entire department dedicated to market research. They also know the local authority's plan for the area concerned.

You can find out about planned transport links or regeneration schemes that are in the pipeline by visiting your local town hall and ask to see the Unitary Development Plan (UDP). This would give you an indication of what the local authority is planning for the area.

(d) Government's Local Policy

Look out for areas undergoing regeneration. An up and coming area is one where the local authority is carrying out regeneration plans such as beautifying houses in the area, improving the streets, creating pavements, streetlights etc. Not only does regeneration create jobs, it also pulls in people and investors. Investing in this area during (or immediately after) regeneration could be beneficial as you would be able to buy at a reasonably low price before competition from other investors pushes up the price.

It is important to note that some local authorities (such as Leeds, Salford, etc.) have now introduced a 'Selective Licensing' policy. This means that if you are a landlord in this area, you would not be able to let out your property unless the property is in a good habitable condition. A licence is then awarded to the landlord permitting him to let his house. Although not many people are happy with this, I feel it would improve the area and would stop landlords from allowing their property to fall into disrepair.

(e) High Yield

Further, some investors look out for areas which offers high yield when determining where to buy. Areas with modest price rise and a strong rental demand is likely to be a high 'rental yield' area.

'Yield' is, by definition, the ratio between rental income and the property value; it is the relationship between the cost of the property and the average annual rent of that property. That is, it is the investor's net rental income expressed as a percentage of the money invested in the property. It converts the rental income into a percentage of the investor's down payment. So, if you invest £60,000 of your own money in a 'quantum property' and you then earn rent of £550 per month (or £6,600 per annum), your 'yield' will be 11%. This means that £6,600 is 11% of your initial investment (namely, £60,000).

If the property is in an area where property prices are high but the average rent earned from property is low, this would result in a low 'rental yield'. To some investors, this would not be the ideal place to invest. However, if the price of the property concerned is modest but the rent earned from that property is high, this would result in a 'high yield'.

Consider this example:

EXAMPLE 6

Joe purchased 10 Drowning Street, London for £450,000. His tenant pays £1,100 as rent per month. What is Joe's yield?

The answer is this:

How to calculate yield (which also means 'Return on Investment') has been covered in chapter 9.

$$\text{Yield} = \frac{\text{Income}}{\text{Property Value/Price}}$$

Yield = £1,100 x 12 months / £450,000

Yield = £13,200 / £450,000

Yield = 0.029 or 2.9%

This means that, assuming there is no void period, investing £450,000 in purchasing 10 Drowning Street would generate 2.9% rental return per annum. In other words, the yield would be 2.9% per annum.

Consider another example:

EXAMPLE 7

Johnson purchased 7 Fishbone Street, Leeds for £85,000. His tenant pays £480 as rent per month. What is Johnson's yield?

The answer is this:

Yield = Income / Property Value/Price

Yield = £480 x 12 months / £85,000

Yield = £5,760 / £85,000

Yield = 0.067 or 6.7%

This means that, assuming there is no void period, investing £85,000 in buying 7 Fishbone Street would generate a yield of 6.7% per annum.

In the first example, the yield was only 2.9% because of the high costs of the property as against the annual rent. However, in the second example, the yield was much higher because of the modest property price.

A recent research carried out by HSBC, which conducted an annual review of rental yields across England and Wales, showed that Manchester, Kingston upon Hull and Blackpool were the best places to invest when considering 'yields'.

***

There appears to be a predictive relationship between yield and property prices. The UK property market has shown that, over time, the more you pay for a property the less your yield is likely to be.

A suggestive heuristic model is to present this in graphical form, which I call the 'Property Rental Yield Curve'.

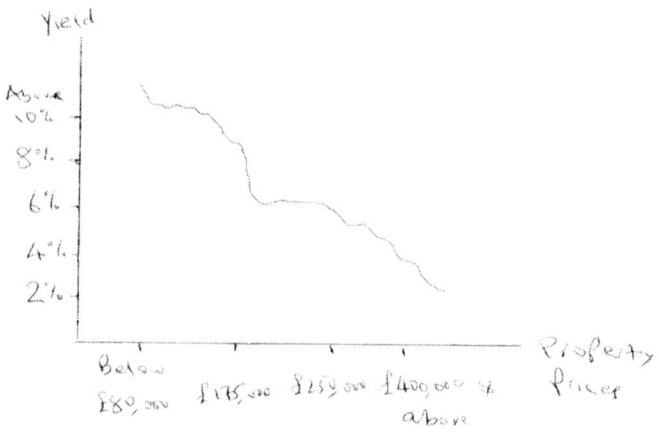

I have plotted the graph above to illustrate the point that, as regards property investment, you are likely to get a higher yield if your outlay (i.e. expenditure) is low by investing in below market value property. As the property price increases, the yield falls. Unlike traditional yield curve, which plots yield of similar quality bonds against their maturity, the 'Property Rental Yield Curve' is 'inverted': this shows that the rental return on investment tends to fall when property prices are relatively high. The 'Property Rental Yield Curve' only applies to investment property.

(f) Capital Appreciation

There are some investors whose investment decision is not influenced by rental yields, but by capital appreciation. Investors with this way of thinking would be looking out for areas where property prices are rising (or rising rapidly). To them, a rising market is an opportunity to buy and sell, making a quick profit in the process.

In the UK, there are areas notorious for rising property prices such as London and the South East of England. However, there are also other areas apart from the South East with rising property prices.

It is, however, important to note that future house price growth is difficult to predict with any certainty. Prices can rise as well as fall. It is therefore prudent to thread carefully when apply the 'capital appreciation' methodology.

Author's Remark

A friend of mine invited me to Manchester during the Commonwealth Games in 2002. I drove around the city and notice some of the areas were run-down but undergoing regeneration. An Estate Agent persuaded me to invest in the area called Clayton. I reluctantly agreed and purchased a 2 bed mid-terrace house for £15,000. I spent £8,000 renovating it and the agent managed it for me. I thought nothing of the property after that.

In 2014, I wanted to remortgage the property so I had it valued. It was valued at £96,000! The regeneration of the Clayton area led to price increase in the area.

CHAPTER 5: WHEN TO INVEST
'Less is more' -Unknown

Determining when to invest is a very important investment factor. 'When to invest' refers to the *timing* of your investment. For example, if you invest in an inflationary market, this would erode your profit, since your aim is to buy 'quantum property' as low as possible and then add value. This is what gives your 'quantum investment' potency.

However, if there are economic conditions creating a downward pressure on property price, this is the time to buy. This is because in a falling market, there are more opportunities. For instance, in a downturn there are always motivated sellers looking to get rid of their property either because of debt or pending repossession. You can pick up a bargain if you time your purchase.

There are a number of factors to take into account when timing your property investment. They are as follows:

- (a) The economy and local property market
- (b) Inflation
- (c) Interest rate
- (d) Consumer confidence index

(a) *__The Economy and Local Property Market__*

Getting to grips with basic 'economics' is fundamental when engaging in property investment.

I know that some people get scared when trying to understand the subject of 'economics'. However, people use 'economics' everyday without knowing it. For instance, when you buy (or plan to buy) a property, you are making an economic decision. Taking out a mortgage involves assessing the interest rates. When the economy contracts and you see wages fall, the effect is felt by tenants and investors alike. There is therefore no getting away from the fact that you must understand basic economics.

You need to assess whether the economy is growing or contracting. If it is contracting, it means that there is unemployment, wages may be falling and there is no spare cash. In such a situation you could buy property below market value.

How do you know when an economy is growing or contracting? The key barometer used to measure the state of the economy is GDP. GDP stands for 'Gross Domestic Product'. GDP measures the value of all goods and services produced in the country. This data can be obtained from the Office for National Statistics (ONS).

The equation used to calculate GDP is:

$$GDP = C + G + I + (X - M)$$

C stands for Consumer Spending
G stands for Government Expenditure
I stands for Investments
X stands for Export
M stands for Import.

Thus, the GDP of a country is the totality of all consumer spending plus government spending plus business investment plus income from export minus expenditure for imports. The total figure arrived at is called the GDP. This represents the size of the economy in any one year.

In order to ascertain how fast an economy is growing, statisticians look at the GDP of one year and compare it with the previous year. The result may show that the GDP grew by, say, 7% or retracted by, say, 4%. If there are 2 or more successive quarterly decline in GDP, the economy would be classified as being in 'recession'.

Economists have identified 4 phases of an economic cycle. The first phase is where the GDP is expanding. Here people are richer. They spend and borrow rashly. The next phase is the peak. Then the economy overheats. Interest rates are hiked. This affects businesses and borrowers, who then cuts back spending, sending the economy into recession. Price falls. This then forms the recipe for a recovery, which is the final phase.

People are more willing to invest when the economy is expanding and there is money floating around. But should you invest when the property market is falling?

My answer is a resounding yes. My reasons are as follows:

First, in an economic downturn there are opportunities. Downturns normally create motivated sellers, who are looking to get rid of their property either because of debt or pending repossession. You can pick up a bargain during this time.

Secondly, economic downturn, by its nature, effectively pushes prices downwards. This means you can buy properties below market value. History has shown that below market value properties tend to rebound during an economic expansion. So, buy these properties with a long-term view.

Land is a scarce resource in the UK. It was Mark Twain who, in the 19th century, said that, "The thing about land is that they are not making any more of it". So, since there is limited supply, any increase in demand for land would increase its price. Simple.

Lastly, in a recession, unemployment is normally high. This means there is likely to be a high supply of properties for sale but with little competition from investors. This creates a buyer's market. Properties bought in these circumstances tend to be bought at a reduced price. This would give you a high rental yield. The high yield is created because you bought at a low price but your rent is high, giving you a good return on your investment.

(b) ***Inflation***

Another factor to take into account when timing your investment is inflation.

Inflation is when too much money is chasing too few goods. It is a period of general rise of the prices for goods and services in any one year.

There are a number of reasons why a nation suffers inflation. An increase in general demand for goods and services without a corresponding increase in supply would lead to price rise, namely inflation. This is called 'Demand-Pull Inflation'. Also, if the high cost of raw materials is being passed on by producers to consumers, this could also lead to inflation. This is known as 'Cost-Push Inflation'. The effect is the same, whether it is demand-pull or cost-push inflation.

If you are looking to buy low value property (i.e. 'quantum property') with a view to adding value by improving the property, then buying during inflation is the wrong move. This is because you would be buying at a higher price.

A deflationary period is ideal. Deflation is the opposite of inflation. This is a period of persistent fall in the general level of prices. At first sight, a period of deflation may create fear amongst some investors. This is because generally, when people see that prices are falling, they tend to delay their spending in the hope that they would get things cheaper. As spending stalls, it weakens the economy.

However, as I have pointed out elsewhere in this book, property prices go up and down. However, if you take a long term view, any property price fall in the long term will rebound upwards. There are a number of reasons for this:

First, there is the constant increase of the UK population, which in turn puts pressure on housing, since people need a place to live. The data from the Office for National Statistics shows that, as at June 2014, the UK population stood at 64.6 million people – a rise of almost half a million since 2013. The number of foreign-born residents living in England and Wales also increased from 4.6 million to 7.5 million since 2001.

Secondly, there is a housing supply shortage in certain areas in the UK, such as London and the South East. In general, local authorities have stopped building houses and are selling off existing council flats. They have left house building to the private sector. Housing developers have said that while they are building more homes, the industry is unlikely to meet government targets. The complex planning rules and procedure; hurdle to surmount when building on cheap brownfield land; and government taxes have all contributed to the shortage of housing. This is causing an upward push on prices.

Thirdly, the number of foreign buyers coming to the UK has increased significantly. This is also pushing up prices.

Fourthly, the government's Help to Buy scheme is pushing price upwards after the credit crunch of 2008. More than 48,000 households have been helped by this scheme. The first phase of the scheme allows people to move on to the property ladder with a deposit of just 5%. Those with 5% deposit can borrow up to 20% of the value of a newly built home from the government in the form of a loan that is interest free for the first 5 years. The second phase of the scheme applies to all properties (old or newly built) provided the cost of the house is less than £600,000. It is available to all. The second scheme works by providing a guarantee whereby the Government would underwrite any loss to the participating banks in the event of repossession.

Lastly, there are some government policies that effectively cause prices to rise. Following a downturn in the economy, governments tend to pursue economic policies to kick-start the economy. For example, after the recession of 2008, the government introduced 'Quantitative Easing' (QE). This effectively is where the central banks are buying government securities or other securities from the market. This mechanism has the effect of increasing the money supply by making cash available to banks, which in turn encourage lending to investors.

Since QE involves injecting money into the economy, it would eventually lead to a rise in inflation and prices would rise.

In view of the above, it can be seen that the time of economic downturn is the best time to search for excellent property deals.

(c) *__Interest Rate__*

Another factor to take into account when timing your investment is interest rate.

When investors talk about interest rate, they almost always refer to the interest rate set by the Central Bank. In the UK, the Bank of England sets the interest rate.

This macroeconomic approach helps to concentrate on how the economy as a whole is doing, rather than looking at a small part of the economy (referred to as microeconomics).

The Bank of England handles the government's monetary policy. This includes managing the money supply, ensuring financial stability, supervising the banking sector and setting the interest rate.

Setting the country's interest rate is one of the most important tools used by the central banks to deal with problems in the economy.

As an investor, you need to know that changing the interest rate could have the following effect:
(a) The interest rate set by the central bank can influence the interest rates private banks charge their borrowers. This influences the interest you pay when you take out a mortgage. If the interest rate is low and you take out a mortgage, the interest you pay the bank is likely to be low, making it the best time to invest in low-value property.
(b) A low interest rate could also have an impact on property prices. A cut in interest rate may lead to lower mortgage rates, which would increase the demand for properties. This effectively would push property prices up.
(c) The changes in interest rate could also effect people's confidence in the economy. Consumer confidence affects how people behave and their spending pattern (see below).

(d) *__Consumer Confidence Index__*

The Consumer Confidence Index is also another economic indicator, used by investors to gauge the sentiments and people's confidence about the economy.

It is a survey conducted to see whether people are optimistic or pessimistic about the state of the economy and how they would conduct their spending for the future.

The idea is that if the consumer is feeling good about the state of the economy, he is more likely to go out and spend. However, if the consumer is feeling pessimistic, he is unlikely to spend. Instead, he would save, thereby compounding the retraction of the economy.

Numerous organisations conduct their own consumer confidence index, such as Lloyds Bank Consumer Confidence index; Nationwide Consumer Confidence index; Deloitte consumer tracker; Clydesdale & Yorkshire; Bank Annual Housebuyers Survey, etc.

However, the UK consumer confidence index is obtained from the finding of the Gfk Consumer Climate Europe Survey, which is conducted on behalf of the European Commission.

When analysing the survey, it is important to note that if the indicator has a positive value, it shows an optimistic viewpoint of the economy. However, if the indicator shows a negative value, then there is pessimism, which means that people are unlikely to spend. This is why this index is an important factor to assess when timing your investment.

However, the point should be made that the consumer confidence index is a lagging indicator; it responds only after the overall economy has already changed. It is a delayed reaction. So do take care when assessing this index.

Author's Remark

Whilst I was presenting at a seminal in London in 2014, one of the attendees told me that, during the recession in 2009, he and his wife purchased 2 mid-terrace properties in Leeds at an auction for £21,000 each. He told me that they would not have been able to buy those properties now that the economy was picking up. He had an eerie smile when he was speaking!

CHAPTER 6: WHAT TO INVEST IN

Another little thing that means a lot – AXA

In this chapter, I would be dealing with what type of residential property to invest in.

There are 5 possible types of residential properties to invest in. They are:

       (a)   Residential houses/flats
       (b)   Student accommodations
       (c)   Holiday let
       (d)   Care homes
       (e)   HMOs

(a) ***Residential Houses/Flats***

These are the typical traditional property, which may be detached, semi detached, terraced or flats. Most residential investors mainly invest in these types of properties. A residential property can be freehold or leasehold.

A freehold residential property, according to property law, is where the property is owned in *fee simply* absolute in possession. This means that the property does not have time limit on its ownership. Unlike leasehold, you are solely responsible for any decisions and maintenance of your property. You have total ownership indefinitely. Also, unlike leasehold properties, you do not pay ground rent.

Another form of land ownership is leasehold. Almost all flats are leasehold. About 21% of UK population live in flats compared to 46% in Sweden.

In a leasehold property, your ownership of a property exists for a specific period of time. The lease may be as short as 21 years or as long as 999 years. Here, there are 2 parties: the landlord and the tenant. The landlord, who is the freeholder, grants a leasehold to the tenant to own the property for certain time. For it to be an 'estate in land', the grant must be more than 21 years but can be as long as 999 years. In return for being granted leasehold title, the tenant must pay rent to the landlord.

In leasehold properties, which are mostly flats, service charges are payable. Service charges are amounts payable for repairs and maintenance for the whole building. It may also cover building insurance and the landlord's cost of managing the property. This clearly shows that the decision about the whole building is not solely yours. Other owners of the other flats share in the decision-making and expense.

Both the landlord and the tenants of the building are bound by the covenant to the lease. The respective obligations and duties of the landlord and tenants of the building are set out in the lease, which is the legal document enforceable in the courts.

The area of leasehold and its operations is a legal minefield. You must seek legal advice when buying a leasehold property.

(b) ***Student Accommodations***

Another class of asset to invest in is student property. Student property has been hailed as a strong asset to invest in. This income generating asset ordinarily offers investors a lower entry level and strong rental returns. Student property is hugely popular and offers regular passive income.

Some towns and cities in the UK are more popular with student let than others. There are areas that are well-known university towns and cities such as Nottingham, London, Manchester, Bristol, Sheffield and Leeds.

If you decide to invest in student property, it is important you consider the following:

1) Choose areas that are safe and secure. The property must be reasonably close to the University.
2) Choose areas that are accessible by rail or road. Parents want their children to be in areas that they can visit with speed and ease.
3) Choose the property with sizeable rooms so that it can contain a desk, bed and wardrobe.
4) Choose properties with reasonable rent so that students with limited budgets could also rent. This would ensure your property is not vacant because of the rent required.

Most local authorities work closely with Universities when it comes to student accommodation. There are some requirements that the investor must adhere to when renting out student properties:

1) The investor must ensure that the property is in a good habitable state.
2) The investor must carry out required repairs when necessary.
3) The investor must ensure that all electrical appliances are safe and the wiring complies with regulation.
4) The investor must ensure that the gas and all gas appliances are checked every 12 months by a suitably, qualified gas engineer.
5) If the student property is furnished, the investor must ensure the furniture is fire resistant and safe.

6) If the property is occupied by 5 or more students, the investor must obtain a licence to let from the local authority. This is because it is a House in Multiple Occupation (HMO). Information about licence procedure can be obtained from the local authority concerned.

When preparing the tenancy agreement with the student tenant, you may consider the following:

1) Make sure the tenancy agreement is an Assured Shorthold Tenancy. The advantage with this form of tenancy is that: (a) you can get your property back from the student-tenant after 6 months if you want; (b) you can ask the court to evict if he owes more than 2 months rent; (c) you can charge the going market rate, etc.
2) Include a clause about nuisance in the agreement.
3) Ensure that the student tenant is aware of the Deposit Scheme, which is responsible for holding the deposit paid by the student.

(c) *Holiday Let*

Another class of asset to invest in is holiday lets. The holiday property market has increased rapidly and can provide good investment opportunity.

In fact, it was established by Direct Line UK Second Property index that in 2006 there were 2.6 million second homes in the UK. The growth of second homes is predicted to increase. Some investors use their second home as holiday lets. As at April 2015, data showed that 6.2% of properties in Cornwall were holiday homes.

If you are considering buying a second home as a holiday let, you should consider the following:

1) Ensure you buy in an area considered as a popular holiday hotspot. The area does not have to be near the beach. For instance, London is a good holiday spot, but is not near the beach.
2) There must be a high demand for property in the area. Places like Blackpool appear to have a glut of properties, which is why there are vacant properties.
3) Ensure there are no environmental issues that could affect your property, such as flooding. You can refer to www.environmentagency.gov.uk for more information.
4) Ensure you have a specialist managing agent to manage the property for you. Endeavour to use an organisation that is part of the National Association of Estate Agents (NAEA), because such organisation is likely to have a Code of Conduct that they adhere to. This organisation would assist you with the lettings requirements, securing tenants, marketing your property, etc.

(d) Care Home

Care homes are another class of asset to invest in. Investment in this area is becoming popular because the number of older people in the UK is increasing. As at June 2014, there were 17.7% of the UK population aged 65 and over. It is estimated that one quarter of people in the UK will be aged 65 and over by 2050. Also, the local authority pays the costs of care for the elderly in care home. Thus, care homes are increasingly seen as high yielding assets with long term, fixed income.

There is a surge of companies investing in the UK care home market. In early 2014, a US hedge fund bought 27 care homes in the UK. Pension funds and insurance companies (such as Aviva and Legal & General) are also investing in this area. Companies also fund new care home developments.

The way investors operate here is that the investor buys a room or unit outright in the development and is promised an annual return of, mostly, 10%. Some developer even promise to buy back the rooms from the investor after 10 years at an agreed price.

This investment can, however, be a risky investment. This is because some areas in the UK are saturated with care homes. As such, some rooms have a low occupancy rate. In the North East, for example, there is an oversupply of care homes.

Secondly, some investors have found that they find it difficult to sell as there is a limited secondary market for piecemeal rooms in a block or building. Others have complained that they are left with onerous management contracts with fees effectively wiping out some or all of their returns on investment.

Lastly, around 430,000 elderly and disabled people live in long-term residential care in the UK. However, 1 in 10 care homes are now in local authority or NHS run institutions. A lot of private companies are entering into this market, but some of them have gone bust. Southern Cross, one of the big players, is an example of a company that failed in this market. Complex and risky financial arrangements are some of the reasons companies have failed here. It can be risky putting your money into this venture without proper due diligence and advice. Seek proper advice before entering this specialist market.

(e) ***HMOs***

Lastly, HMOs are another class of asset to invest in. HMO stands for House in Multiple Occupation. A property would be classified as an HMO if it is rented out to at least

3 or more people (who are not from the same family), but share facilities such as kitchen and bathroom.

Investors looking to invest in HMOs must obtain a licence from the local authority where the property is located. An HMO cannot be rented out without a licence. The process of obtaining a licence is available at the local authority where the property is. You can be fined up to £20,000 for renting out an unlicensed HMO. A licence is valid for 5 years.

The main reason people invest in HMOs is because of the rental returns this investment generates. HMO creates a multiple steam of passive income. If you invest in an HMO with, say, 3 bedsits, this would generate 3 sources of rents. The arithmetic to measure whether or not an HMO is profitable is covered in chapter 9.

There is plenty of help available online on HMOs. Some of the helpful websites are:
www.nationalhmonetwork.com; www.pims.co.uk; www.hmohub.co.uk; www.hmodaddy.com; etc. You can also find bargain HMOs for sale online. Some of the useful websites can be seen in Appendix ii.

CHAPTER 7: HOW TO INVEST/RAISING FUNDS

Small things come in great sizes - Unknown

It is not in any doubt that property prices are rising in the UK. In fact the Treasury forecast that house prices are expected to rise by 31.4% by the first quarter of 2020. According to Halifax, the average property price now stands at £186,941. The increase in property price is making it difficult for some investors to enter the UK property market.

In order to be able to invest, it is important to be able to raise funds. Savvy investors have mastered the art of raising funds to facilitate the purchase of property. They understand the various ways funds can be raised. However, the various sources of funds are rather mundane once you get to understand them. ***You can even acquire property with no money down!*** Here, I would set out various ways funds could be raised for property investments.

There are 17 separate ways funds could be raised for property investments. They are as follows:

1) Income
2) Savings (including ISA)
3) Mortgage (buy-to-let)
4) Pension Fund
5) Gifts or inheritances
6) Selling Unproductive Assets
7) Further Advance
8) Equity Release/Re-Mortgaging
9) Novation
10) Second Charge
11) Unsecured Loan

12) Help to Buy
13) Rent to Buy
14) Split Title
15) Shared Ownership & Staircasing
16) Joint Ownership
17) Overage

1) Income

One way to raise funds is from your income. There are 3 types of income: earned income; passive income and financial product income.

The first type of income from which investment fund can be raised is from earned income. These are earnings from employment (or self-employment); or income from referral fees as a result of sourcing properties for someone else, who in turn pays you for it; or income from renting out a room in your home (although you need the lenders consent, if you have a mortgage on the property), etc.

Another type of income is passive income. This is income generated from your other investment property. The rent received from tenant is passive income. This income can be added to your earned income and used as the investment fund to acquire property.

Financial product income is another source of fund, which can be used to acquire property. Financial product income is income generated from investments in stocks & shares, derivatives, bond, etc.

2) Savings (including ISA)

Another way to fund your property investment is by using your savings. If you find that your savings are insufficient, you may consider utilising your Instant Savings Accounts

(ISA), if there is one. Bear in mind that some ISA such as Halifax Saver Fixed ISA, which requires a savings of up to £15,000, cannot be withdrawn except you wish to close the account. Do take professional advice before embarking on any withdrawals since there are different types of ISAs.

3) Mortgage (Buy-to-let)

Obtaining a mortgage is another way to fund your property investment. A mortgage, which is primarily taken out solely to acquire investment property for the rental market, is known as a 'buy-to-let' (**BTL**) mortgage.

The BTL loans have grown rapidly since it was introduced in 1996. There are now more than 700 BTL mortgage deals available to investors. In 2013, more than £20 billion was lent to investors, and this is predicted to increase substantially in the coming years!

However, in 2014 the Government introduced stricter lending criteria for BTL investors to satisfy, referred to as the Mortgage Market Review (**MMR**). The aim of the new mortgage affordability rules is to 'stress test' how much an investor can borrow. So, what can an investor do to increase his chances of getting a mortgage?

Step 1: Do your homework

It is prudent to seek advice from a specialist BTL mortgage broker. However, before meeting your broker, your first step is to work out how much deposit you can raise from your savings or income. The size of your deposit affects your mortgage affordability. It also affects the mortgage rates available to you: if the loan to value is low, the lender is taking less risk. This gets you a better mortgage rate.

When assessing a mortgage application, BTL lenders do check the investor's credit report to give a credit score. Therefore, before you make your mortgage application, it is important to check your credit report to ensure it is accurate and up to date. You may use Experian to check your credit report.

Step 2: Find a Mortgage Broker

Although as an investor, you can just walk into your bank or building society and ask for a mortgage, however, the bank will only sell their own products to you. Getting advice from a broker will give you access to more mortgage products, which, in turn, is likely to get you the best rates.

The BTL mortgage broker will need information about your income and expenditure in order to find the best mortgage deals for you. When meeting your broker, you need the following:

- Photographic ID (e.g. passport, Driver's Licence, etc.)
- Proof of address: such as utility bills in the last 3 months
- Proof of income: 3 months wage slips (or if self employed, 3 years set of accounts)
- Last 3 months bank statements
- Proof that you do not have immigration restrictions

At the meeting, the broker will use his specialist software to find the best mortgage rates for you. A broker will also suggest the mortgage product suitable for you. There are different types of mortgages and mortgage products:

- (a.) Interest Only Mortgage
- (b.) Repayment Mortgage
- (c.) Fixed Rate Mortgage

(d.) Tracker Mortgage
(e.) Offset Mortgage.

Interest Only Mortgage: Here, you are only paying the interest on the loan. The full mortgage loan would need to be repaid at the end of the mortgage term (which may be a 25 year term).

Repayment Mortgage: Here, you are paying the interest and reducing the loan by each monthly payment made.

Fixed Rate Mortgage: This type of mortgage set interest rate at a fixed level for period of time (usually between 1 to 10 years). This means you would pay exact amount each month irrespective of whether the Bank of England base rate goes up or down.

Tracker Mortgage: Here, the interest you pay is linked to the Bank of England base rate. So, if the Bank of England base rate is reduced, then your mortgage rate would also fall, but a base rate hike would lead to an increase of your mortgage rate. You are therefore at the mercy of the Monetary Policy Committee (MPC) of the Bank of England, who meets regularly to determine the base rate.

Offset Mortgage: This type of mortgage combines your savings account with your mortgage account under one account. Thus, any money in your savings account goes towards reducing your mortgage. For example, if you have a mortgage of £85,000 and savings of £25,000, you will only pay interest on £60,000 of the loan.

Step 3: Lender's Decision

At the meeting with your broker, the broker would carry out fact-finding and come up with a suitable mortgage product. You would then be required to choose whether you wish to go ahead with that lender and mortgage product. Your broker would then prepare and submit your application to the lender.

The mortgage lender will go through the application and examine the supporting documentation (which contains your ID, proof of income and address, etc). They will then run a credit check to see if you have a poor credit history or County Court Judgment (CCJ). If satisfied, the lender would instruct a valuer to value the property you are looking to buy.

It is important to be aware that some lenders may not lend: (a) to investors over a certain age; or (b) if the flat is above the 5th floor; or (c) if the freeholder of the block of flats cannot be found; or (d) if the property is above commercial premises.

Step 4: Instruct a Solicitor

During your mortgage application process, you would be required to appoint a firm of solicitors to carry out the conveyancing once the mortgage is approved.

Some lenders would only use law firms on their 'Panel'. Check with your solicitor whether they are on the lender's panel before nominating them as your lawyer.

Step 5: The Mortgage Offer

If the lender is satisfied with your application and the Valuation Report, they will then issue a mortgage offer to you. This is the ticket that would give you access to the property investment market! A copy of the mortgage offer would also be sent to your solicitor.

4) Pension Funds and Annuity

The rules on pension are changing. Since April 2015, if you are 55 years or older you can now withdraw part or all your money from the pension pot. If you choose to take your money in this way, 25% is tax-free and the remaining 75% is taxable. Assuming you have £60,000 in the pot, you can take £15,000 tax-free. The remaining £45,000 would be taxable.

If you are considering taking money out of your pot, you need to consider how you can utilise the money in such as way that it gives you an income when you retire. Make sure you speak to a registered financial adviser if you are looking to reinvest your money.

Annuities are also another source of funds. An annuity is an insurance policy that gives you guaranteed income for the rest of your life. There are different types of annuities. From April 2016, people who are drawing an annuity will be able to sell that income to a third party for a capital sum. This effectively would allow annuity holders to sell their annuities without punitive penalties of up to 70%.

5) Gifts and Inheritances

Another way to raise money is by selling your unproductive gifts or inheritances. You need to be sure that you would get a better return in property investment before deciding to sell. Further, there are some gifts or inheritances that have sentimental value. You need to consider this factor as well.

6) Selling Unproductive Assets

You may have other assets you may have acquired. Again, if you feel that they are unproductive, then you may sell them and raise funds from the proceeds towards purchasing investment property.

7) Further Advances

One key way to raise cash, if you already have a mortgage, is to approach your mortgage lender and ask for an additional loan secured against the same property. This would generate you more cash to invest in another investment property.

If you decide to go down this road to raise cash, your mortgage lender may assess your monthly income and expenditure to determine your ability to repay the loan. You would also be responsible for the cost of obtaining a valuation report from a surveyor and solicitor's conveyancing fees.

Since further advance increases your loan with the lender, you are effectively increasing your level of debt and your monthly repayment obligation. Make sure you work out what your repayment would be and that you would be able to make the repayment with some ease. Make sure that the yield from the new property investment justifies taking out this additional loan. You may find it useful to refer to *Maths for Buyers and Sellers* in chapter 9.

8) Equity Releases/Re-Mortgaging

Another fund-raising exercise is 'equity release' or 're-mortgaging'. Re-mortgaging occurs where a borrower switches his loan from the old lender to the new lender with a view to releasing equity in a property.

One reason why buy-to-let (**BTL**) re-mortgage is increasingly becoming popular is because it allows investors to use their existing property to raise extra cash to fund more investment, thereby expanding their property portfolio.

Before obtaining a BTL re-mortgage, ensure that the rent from the property you are looking to buy offers a big enough margin over the new mortgage payments. Secondly, ensure the rates are reasonable and the loan-to-value (LTV) is reasonably high, otherwise you may not be able to release the equity you need for your investment.

When arranging a switch of mortgage lenders, make sure you speak to a mortgage broker, who would help you find lenders with excellent rates.

In addition, there are free websites available that would enable you compare mortgage rates with other banks so as to find out which rates are lower. One such websites is www.loans-hub.com/mortgages

When meeting your broker, endeavour to take with you the redemption figure from the existing lender. A 'redemption figure' tells you how much you owe your existing lender.

Almost all BTL lenders apply the rental stress tests; investors would need to demonstrate that the rental income covers the monthly repayment.

When processing your application, some lenders charge up to 2.5% of the amount of the re-mortgage loan to arrange the mortgage. You would also be responsible for the cost of valuation and solicitor's conveyancing fees.

9) Novation

Novation is an aspect of the Law of Contract, which allows a debt repayment obligation under a mortgage to be transferred from the previous borrower to another party in return for which the lender releases the previous borrower from the mortgage. The new party becomes the borrower under the same terms as the previous agreement.

There are various reasons why a borrower may wish to get out of a mortgage with the lender:

- property is about to be repossessed;
- loss of job;
- saddled with debt and wishes to free himself;
- serious illness;
- old and frail;
- seriously disabled;
- getting cash in return for novation, etc.

If you are using this method to acquire property, you must also take steps to register your title with the Land Registry (if this is what is agreed with the previous borrower). This is because the novation agreement does not transfer property. It merely affects the mortgage obligations.

You need to know that some lender may not consent to the novation. So you must get the borrower to check with his lender first before embarking on this journey. If all the parties consent, you must speak to a solicitor, since this is a specialist area.

10) Second Charge

You can also raise extra cash for investment by taking out a second mortgage against your existing property. A second charge loan occurs where a second lender advances a loan and takes the property as security but the second loan is inferior to the first existing mortgage.

If you decide to go down this road to raise cash, your second mortgage lender may assess your monthly income and expenditure to determine your ability to repay the additional loan. You would also the responsible for the cost of obtaining a valuation report from a surveyor and solicitor's conveyancing fees.

Since a second charge loan effectively increases your loan amount with both lenders, you are effectively increasing your level of debt and your monthly repayment obligation. Make sure you work out what your additional repayment would be and that you would be able to make the payment with some ease. Also, make sure that the yield from the new property investment funded by the second charge loan justifies taking out this additional loan. You may find the Loan to Rent (LTR) ratio in chapter 9 useful when doing your calculation as to the affordability of a second loan.

Some second charge lenders are reluctant to lend to some investors because of the 'overreaching' principles, which applies in property transactions. 'Overreaching' is a concept in English land law which stems from the provision of section 2(1) of the **Law of Property Act 1925**. It operates where, for example, a first mortgagee repossesses property which has a second mortgage. The second chargee may get nothing if the proceed of sale is insufficient to cover the first mortgage. The new buyer gets the property free from the second charge (even if it was registered with the Land Registry). See also the case of ***City of London Building Society v Flegg [1988] AC 54***.

11) Unsecured Loan

Another way to raise funds for your property investment is by taking out an unsecured loan.

You can take out a loan from banks, other financial institution, family and friends.

Before taking any loan, ensure that you prepare an income and expenditure plan and a cash flow forecast to ensure you can repay the loan. Also try and secure the most favourable terms for the loan as possible (e.g. low interest rates; reasonable duration to repay, etc.) Make sure that the rental return from the likely investment would cover the monthly loan repayment with excess for you to benefit from. The arithmetic to assess whether the rental income would sufficiently cover the loan is covered in chapter 9 (see example 13).

12) Help to Buy

The Help to Buy mortgage support scheme is there to help people looking to buy property they would live in. The scheme does not apply to properties to be rented out. It is therefore of no use to investors looking to build up property portfolios.

13) Rent to Buy

There are people who although have a bad credit history nonetheless wish to buy property. Such people can use the Rent to Buy Scheme. The Rent to Buy Scheme is a private scheme run by various private organisations turning tenants into property owners.

The scheme is designed for people with a bad credit history and also unable to raise the initial deposit for purchase of a property. The scheme gives the tenant/buyer time to rectify his credit history whilst occupying the property.

The Rent to Buy Scheme works as follows: First, you search for property being sold under the Rent to Buy Scheme. You can find some properties at www.nationalpropertygroup.co.uk or www.renttobuy-homes.co.uk

Secondly, you then enter into a Rent to Buy contract with the landlord/seller whereby you pay rent plus a monthly 'deposit top up' to the Landlord/seller for the agreed period (which could be between 5 years and 10 years) at a given sale price. This allows you to build up your deposit to be used to purchase the house on the agreed date.

Upon the agreed date, the deposit is used toward the purchase of the house, but you must obtain a mortgage for the balance.

The tenant/buyer has all the benefit of a home-owner; so you can sell the property anytime before the agreed date to another buyer and you can keep the surplus gained over and above the agreed price with the landlord/seller. Prior to any sale, you are responsible for maintaining the house.

It is important to note the following:

> (a) if you buy a property under this scheme and you fail to get a mortgage after the agreed period, you may forfeit your deposit;
> (b) if you agree with the landlord-seller to buy the house within 5 years but you complete after 5 years, you may be responsible for any increase in price; and
> (c) if you fail to pay the rent and/or the 'deposit top up', the house may be at risk in the same way as failing to pay your mortgage. If you are in arrears of more than 2 months, the tenancy could be terminated and you would lose your deposit.

14) Split Title

If you have a house on a large plot of land, you can raise fund by selling off a portion of the land. This can be achieved by splitting the title. In order to enhance the sale, you can apply for planning permission before selling. This would increase the value of the portion of land you are selling.

When taking this decision, it is vital that you ascertain whether it is better to build on the land as opposed to selling. However, if you feel you could get something better which gives a better return, then you may sell.

Remember that landlocked properties are more difficult to sell than ones where access is not a problem. Lastly, once you sell the land, you do not know who your neighbours are going to be in future. So do consider this.

15) Shared Ownership & Staircasing

For investors with insufficient funds, one way of getting on the property ladder is by shared ownership and subsequently, staircasing.

Shared ownership arises when you buy or own a certain percentage in a property and you pay rent for the other part to the landlord. You may own 25% share in the property and your landlord owns 75%.

Shared ownership is meant to be a stepping-stone to outright ownership of property.

A key element of mobility for shared ownership is 'staircasing'. 'Staircasing' is a term used to describe the process of buying extra shares in your shared ownership property. This allows you to go up another step on the home ownership ladder by buying further shares.

In order to take the first step into shared ownership, you need to try and search for properties being sold as shared ownership. You may visit www.helptobuynesh.co.uk. Secondly, speak to a financial adviser for advice on loans, if applicable.

If you own a shared ownership property and want to staircase, you must first contact you mortgage lender, if applicable, about further lending.

Remember that you can buy about 25% or more of the shares at the current market value, disregarding any improvement to your home that the landlord has consented to. Also, you are responsible for the cost of valuing the property together with any legal costs associated with the transaction.

16) Joint Ownership

You can team up with someone else to invest in property so that you do not have to raise all the money. This is known as 'joint ownership'.

When you opt for joint ownership house, you share the deposit, there is a joint mortgage application, joint mortgage payments, and joint household bills.

If you are considering joint ownership, you should get advice about the joint mortgage application from a registered financial adviser.

It is also important to decide what type of joint ownership you want.

An investment property jointly owned can be held either as *joint tenants* or *tenants-in-common*.

Joint Tenancy:
If you buy property with someone else as 'joint tenancy', this means that when one of the owners dies, the other surviving owner automatically owns the entire property. If this is not what you want and the property has already been purchased, then you can serve a Notice of Severance on the other owner making it clear that you intent to sever the joint tenancy. Once this is properly done, then the 'joint tenancy' would become 'tenancy-in-common'.

Tenancy-in-Common:
In this type of agreement, each of the owners own a separate share in the property. So if one of the owners dies, his share will not pass to the survivor. Instead, his share would pass to whoever he has mentioned in his will.

So if you want to buy an investment property with someone else and would wish to pass your share in the investment property to your children, then 'tenancy-in-common' is the best type of ownership for reasons given above. Ensure you seek legal advice if you are opting for joint ownership

17) Overage

An investor looking to get on the property ladder and any seller hoping to raise quick cash can both utilise the 'overage' arrangement. What is 'overage'?

An 'overage' is a provision written into a contract of sale of land or property sold at undervalue. It describes the situation where a seller sells his land at a low value and then contract to receive a percentage of the uplift when the land is eventually developed and sold by the buyer.

In other words, 'overage' refers to a situation where a seller, having sold his property to the buyer at a reduced price, retains his right to share in the future increased value of the land after being improved/developed by the buyer.

Both parties benefit from the overage arrangement in that the buyer acquires at a reduced price and the seller retains his right to share future profit as a result of improvement to the land (which included obtaining planning permission).

If you wish to engage in an overage arrangement, you can market your property as such. You must seek legal advice as this is a complicated area of contract law. Your solicitor would negotiate on your behalf, draft the contract and register a RESTRICTION or CHARGE on the title at the Land Registry. The overage provision in the contract would stipulate what triggers payment and how much.

It is important to note that not all lenders would lend in an overage transaction. Secondly, this arrangement can be quite costly as it involves surveyors and solicitors costs. Thirdly, the buyer is responsible for paying the stamp duty. Lastly, if a seller puts a RESTRICTION on the title to the property at the Land Registry, and the seller cannot be found, this may delay the eventual sale by the buyer.

Author's Remark

In late 2013, I was looking to invest in areas outside London undergoing regeneration. Someone then told me about Hull. I called Hull City Council and was told of the areas undergoing regeneration. I drove to the areas and saw a 2 bed end terrace being sold for £21,500. I only had £10,000 at the time. So I teamed up with my brother and we both purchased the property jointly. Shortly afterwards, the local authority regenerated the entire street. I would not have been able to buy that property at that time and for that price without the joint venture.

CHAPTER 8: PURCHASING WITH NO MONEY DOWN

'Nothing in all the world is more dangerous than sincere ignorance'
– Martin Luther King Jr

INTRODUCTION

In chapter 7, I covered the various ways funds could be raised with a view to investing in property. There are however certain circumstances when you are unable to raise funds. In such circumstances, you can still invest in property without putting down any of your money. The ability to do this offers the savvy investor another opportunity to increase his 'energy' of profit by leveraging.

Before exploring how you can buy with no money down, it is essential to note the following: investing with no money down would be of little effect unless you can find and buy below market value (BMV) or distressed property. The saying goes that *you make money when you buy, not when you sell.* This is because if you manage to buy at a bargain, this instantly gives you equity in the property, which you can release when you sell.

Thus, there are different types of bargain properties you can buy:

i. Distressed properties, which needs full repairs
ii. Inherited property, where the beneficiary is looking for a quick sale
iii. Divorced sellers looking to quickly sell
iv. Tired landlords looking to sell
v. Emigrating seller
vi. Sellers with serious ill-health
vii. Relocating sellers

viii. Repossessed property
ix. Motivated seller in financial difficulty
x. Property with defective title: This type of property is notoriously difficult to sell. For this reason, sellers are willing to drop their prices substantially. An intelligent buyer should be purchasing this kind of property. Your solicitor can then rectify the defective title or obtain indemnity insurance to deal with the problem. However, ensure you obtain legal advice before buying such property. Secondly, banks might not lend against such a property. So, the purchase might have to be a cash purchase, but for a bargain.

STRATEGIES

There are a number of ways an investor can buy BMV property without putting down any of his own money. They are:

(a) Peer-2-peer arrangement
(b) Novation/assumption of existing mortgage
(c) Lease option
(d) Instalment contract

(a) Peer-2-Peer

The key way to buy property with no money down is to partner with a friend or colleague who has cash but does not want the inconvenience of owning property. Both parties can jointly work together where the individual lender lends to the property investor either in return for periodic interest payment (until the loan is repaid) or a share in the profit when the property is sold. The property investor would be responsible for the day-to-day management of the project.

So, armed with money from the peer-2-peer lender, the property investor can then invest in suitable property without putting down any of his own money. However, if there is a shortfall and the investor is looking to take out a mortgage for the balance, then the investor must notify the mortgage company that the deposit is coming from his business partner.

A property investor can find a P-2-P lender either from his sphere of influence or by using P-2-P companies.

It is advisable that anyone looking to engage in P-2-P arrangement should prepare a partnership agreement. It is important to obtain legal advice when drafting the partnership agreement. The agreement should cover the responsibilities of the parties, interest payment or fee sharing, whose name should be on the title deeds and how the agreement can be terminated, etc. Any partnership agreement is subject to the provisions of the **Partnership Act 1890**.

(b) Novation/Assumption of Existing Mortgage

Another means of buying property with no money down is by Novation. I have already covered this in chapter 7 above.

(c) Lease Option

There are situations when a seller is desperate to sell his property either because he is looking to relocate or being unable to make monthly repayment of the mortgage. This creates the reason for a seller to accept a 'Lease Option'.

A lease option agreement is also known as rent-to-buy. It allows an investor to rent a property from a seller with a choice (i.e. option) to buy the property from the seller at a price agreed earlier when the option was created.

Lease options are already well known is the US, Australia and other overseas property markets. They are, however, relatively new in the UK property market. There are now numerous property companies offering lease options as a way of getting on to – off- the property ladder. 'Option fees', which is an upfront payment to set up the property deal, goes for as little as £1. This has led many lease option companies declaring that 'investors can now buy a property for £1'.

How does it work?

A lease option involves an investor agreeing to rent a property from the Seller with an **option** to buy the property for the price of, say, £100,000 within 5 years. The rent the investor pays the seller includes the cost of the monthly mortgage payment, any building insurance payment (and, if the property is leasehold, service charge and ground rent). Any surplus rent payments are credited towards the purchase price if the investor negotiates with the Seller that they are to act as the investor's 'deposit'. The seller may charge for the **option**. Some investors pay as little as £1. The option may be for any period up to a maximum of 18 years.

At the end of the option, the investor may obtain a mortgage for the balance due to the seller.

Thus, a lease option allows an investor to delay completion whilst having full control of a property.

How can you purchase with no money down?
There are numerous strategies an investor can employ when utilising a lease option.

The first strategy is this:

Step 1: Find a seller looking to sell with an option.

Step 2: Negotiate the sale price with the seller and pay as little as possible for the option. Ensure that a proportion of the rent you pay the seller prior to buying the property goes towards the purchase price as a 'deposit'. Ensure you ask for a longer option period to give you time to raise the mortgage in due course.

Step 3: Negotiate with the seller to allow you to rent out the property. Obtain a Power of Attorney from the seller granting you authority to let the property under an Assured Shorthold Tenancy Agreement.

Step 4: Get the lease option agreement and the Power of Attorney drafted by a solicitor. Have those documents signed by the seller, which effectively gives possession of the property to you.

Step 5: Rent out the property to another tenant. Ensure that the rent sufficiently covers the amount you are supposed to pay the seller, plus something extra for you.

Step 6: Towards the end of the option, obtain a mortgage for the balance and complete the purchase.

From the above, you would have purchased the property without putting down any money: you would have had possession of the property from the seller, rent it to another tenant and the rent this new tenant pays goes towards your deposit.

The second strategy is this:

Rather than wait to exercise the option, you can sell the option before the due date.

EXAMPLE 8

Let us say Tim is a property investor, who is looking to rent-to-buy a property worth £120,000 in June 2015. Assuming the Option price is £135,000 to be exercised on or before June 2020. If soaring prices bring the value of the property to £175,000 as at today, Tim can sell his Option before the due date for £40,000 (i.e. the difference between £175,000 and £135,000) to another investor.

A lease option not only allows investors to grow their portfolio, it also allows them to rent out a property and generate rental income before they own the property.

In spite of the benefits of using lease options, investors must tread carefully. Firstly, some lenders may not approve lease options. Ensure that the seller speaks to his lenders for permission before embarking on this journey.

Secondly, a lease option is not completely free of risk. In the example above, if the value of the property end up falling over the period of the option, Tim would be left with either purchasing the property at a higher price or forfeit his option to buy. This means that Tim would have lost out because of the wasted rent payments.

(d) Instalment Contract

Instalment Contracts offers investors an alternative way of purchasing property with no money down. An instalment contract is a contract for the sale of property where the seller agrees to accept instalment payments from the buyer until the full amount has been paid. Under an instalment contract, the seller retains the legal title to the property, while permitting the buyer to take possession of it, until the full price has been paid.

How can you invest with no money down under an instalment contract?
The whole essence of an instalment contract is for the investor to make instalment payments to the seller whilst the investor is in occupation of the property. It does not matter who makes the payment, provided the payments are up-to-date. As such, the investor has the liberty of letting out the property; the rent received can then be paid over to the seller as the instalment payment. By so doing, the investor is purchasing property with none of his money down.

An investor looking to utilise the instalment contract method must ensure that his solicitor protect the arrangement after the agreement has been entered into with the seller. The solicitor acting for the investor can protect this agreement by applying for a restriction on the register using Form RX1. The application must set out full details of the basis for the application. The application is made to Her Majesty's Land Registry and a fee is payable. This would prevent any recalcitrant seller from secretly entering into another instalment contract with another party.

It is important to note that instalment contracts are not totally without risks. One major concern is that if, having collected the payments from the investor-buyer, the seller fails to make the mortgage payments, the property could be repossessed by the Bank, which would mean that the investor would lose all the payments he has made thus far.

Another concern is that if the seller has a mortgage on the property, the lender may not consent to the instalment contract arrangement with the investor.

In order to address the above drawbacks, any investor looking to utilise instalment contract must insist that the seller obtain permission from his lender prior to entering into the instalment contract with the investor. This can be included as a condition in the contract. At common law, a breach of a condition allows the innocent party to rescind the contract.

Secondly, the investor must request that the seller insert a clause in the instalment contract that the seller shall give quarterly disclosure to the investor of the mortgage payment by disclosing the mortgage statements. This clause would allow the investor monitor the mortgage account.

CHAPTER 9: THE MATHEMATICS OF PROPERTY INVESTMENTS

Ipsa scientia potestas est (knowledge itself is power)

INTRODUCTION

This chapter examines the aspect of mathematics, which affects property transactions and investments.

The problem-solving logic of mathematics lends itself as a useful tool to the property investor. Every time you work out your rates of return on your investments, you are doing maths. When you add, subtract, multiply or divide, you are at the heart of mathematics.

Even algebra can be a useful tool for the property investor. Consider this example:

EXAMPLE 9

Joe is thinking of buying a property. He has allocated £10,000 for renovation but does not want to exceed a budget of £175,000 as total expenditure. How much should he spend to buy the property?

This involves algebra. Since we do not know the purchase price, we will use 'Y' to represent the 'unknown'. The calculation goes as follows:

Y + £10,000 = £175,000

Y = £175,000 - £10,000

Y = £165,000

Joe must spend no more than £165,000 (as the purchase price) to ensure he does not exceed his budget. Simple.

Let us consider another example to illustrate the usefulness of maths to the property investor.

EXAMPLE 10

Tony and Joe purchased 16 Green Acre for £135,000. It was agreed that if the property was to be sold, Tony was to be entitled to £23,000 more than Joe from any profit made. Assuming the property sold for £267,000, how is profit to be shared?

Using algebra would be of help here.

Let us have a go:

£267,000 - £135,000 = £132,000 profit.

So, when the profit of £132,000 is being shared, Tony must receive £23,000 more than Joe's share.

Tony's share (**T**) + Joe's share (**J**) = £132,000

$$T+J = £132,000$$
$$T-J = £23,000$$
$$2T = £155,000$$

$$T = \frac{£155,000}{2}$$
$$T = £77,500$$

Tony's share = £77,500
Joe's share = £54,500
£77,500 + £54,500 = £132,000

So Tony's share would be £77,500 and Joe's share would be £54,500; this makes Tony's share £23,000 more than Joe's.

You can see from these examples that understanding mathematics is crucial as a property investor.

++

In this section, I will deal with the following:

(1) Maths for buyer and seller
(2) Maths for HMOs
(3) Maths for overage
(4) Maths for novation
(5) Maths for shared ownership

(1) <u>MATHS FOR BUYER and SELLER</u>

Under this heading, we will examine the following

(i) Calculating loan to value (LTV) ratio
(ii) Calculating loan to rent (LTR) ratio
(iii) Maths involving joint purchasers
(iv) Calculating income, yield and price
(v) Calculating estate agent's commission

(i) Loan to Value (LTV)

The LTV deals with the portion of the purchase price that a lender is willing to lend. If the lender is willing to cover 85% of the purchase price, then the buyer must raise 15% of the purchase price from his income or savings.

The formula for calculating LTV is:

$$LTV = \frac{Loan}{Price}$$

Consider this example:

EXAMPLE 11

A property was purchased with a deposit of £25,000 and a loan of £185,000 at 4.5% for 25 years. What is the LTV ratio?

The answer is:

The formula for LTV ratio = $\frac{Loan}{Price}$

The purchase price is £25,000 + £185,000 = £210,000

LTV ratio = $\frac{£185,000}{£210,000}$

LTV ratio = 88%

Here, this means that the lender is willing to lend 88% of the purchase price to the investor. The investor must, however, raise 12% of purchase price from his own source.

EXAMPLE 12

Broohday Bank Plc agreed to lend Joe 85% of the purchase price. As a result, Joe puts down £25,000 as his deposit. What is the purchase price?

The answer is this:

$85^{\%}$ + £25,000 = Purchase Price

£25,000 = 15% of Purchase Price

$$\frac{25,000}{15\%} = £166,666.$$

The purchase price is £166,666.

(ii) Loan to Rent (LTR)

The LTR deals with the portion of the rental income eaten up by the monthly mortgage repayment. *This only applies to rental property.* Thus, if the mortgage repayment eats up 90% of the rental income, it therefore means that the investor is only left with 10% of the rent as his income.

It is prudent to ensure that the rent from the property you are looking to buy covers the amount needed for the mortgage repayment. Be clinical when assessing this.

The formula for calculating LTR is:

LTR = Loan
         Rent

Consider this example

EXAMPLE 13

The rent for the property at 17 Malachi Road is £750 per month. The monthly mortgage payment is £550. What is the LTR ratio?

The answer is:

The formula for LTR ratio = Loan
                                                Rent

$$\text{LTR} = \frac{£550}{£750} = 0.73$$

LTR ratio = 73%

This means that 73% of the rent goes towards paying the monthly mortgage; the investor is only retaining 27% of the rent as his income.

It is important to note that the less you have left after paying the mortgage, the more exposed you are to defaulting on the mortgage in the event of a rate hike. *Sumptus censum ne superet* (let not your spending exceed your income).

Thus, a lower LTR ratio not only guarantees that the rent would sufficiently cover the mortgage in the event of a rate hike, it would also ensure that over time the excess income accumulated and retained by the investor can be used as a deposit for more investment. See 'Velocity' in chapter 2.

Investing in 'quantum property' as advocated in this book, reduces the risk of a high LTR ratio, since this entails buying BMV property.

(iii) Maths involving joint purchasers:
The law affecting joint purchasers has been covered in chapter 7. However, being able to work out each party's share is very important.

Consider the following example:

EXAMPLE 14

Tony purchased 21 Read Acre Road with 7 other friends. Everyone contributed equal amounts including Tony, who contributed £30,000. What was the purchase price?

The answer is this:

If everyone contributed an equal amount, then they each contributed £30,000.

£30,000 x 8 = £240,000

In this example, giving that there are 8 joint owners, only 4 of them can have their names on the land register of this property at the Land Registry. These 4 registered proprietors would then be treated as '**trustees**', who would be holding this property on trust for themselves and the others, who are **beneficiaries**.

EXAMPLE 15

Tony bought 16 Green Acre with 3 others. Tony contributed £32,000 for a 3/8 share. What is the cost of the property?

The answer is this:

£32,000 = $3/8$ of purchase price

If you covert $3/8$ into a percentage, you will get 37.5%

So £32,000 = 37.5% of the purchase price

Purchase Price = $\underline{£32,000}$
                    37.5%

Purchase Price = £85,333.33

(iv) Calculating income, yields and price:

The key purpose of an investment is to generate profit. Therefore being able to calculate the percentage or monetary amount of profit (or loss) is important. Remember that a 'profit' is how much you make over and above your expenditure. It may be expressed as a percentage or as an amount.

Consider this example:

EXAMPLE 16

Tony purchased 16 Green Acre for £185,000 and sold it for £210,000, giving him a profit of £25,000. What is the percentage of his profit?

The calculation goes as follows:

The formula is: How much you made divide by the original cost paid. The formula can be expressed as:

MADE
PAID

Percentage of profit = $\dfrac{£25,000}{£185,000}$

$$= 0.135135$$

To change this decimal figure to a percentage, move the decimal point two places to the right and add the percentage sign (%). Or you multiply the decimal number by 100. It would arrive at the same thing.

So the percentage of profit is: 13.5%

Consider this example:

EXAMPLE 17

Andrea purchased 4 Valkov Street for £245,000. She spent £9,500 on renovation and sold the property for £274,950. What is the percentage of her profit?

The formula here is: $\dfrac{\text{PROFIT MADE}}{\text{TOTAL OUTLAY}}$

The total amount initially invested (i.e. her total outlay) = £245,000 + £9,500 = £254,500

Andrea made: £274,950 - £254,500 = £20,450 profit

The percentage profit = $\dfrac{£20{,}450}{£254{,}500}$

The percentage profit = .0803 or 8%. So Andrea made 8% profit from the sale of her property.

Consider this example:

EXAMPLE 18

Tony purchased 16 Green Acre for £185,000 and sold it at a loss for £145,000, giving him a loss of £40,000. What is the percentage of his loss?

The formula is: $\dfrac{\text{Loss}}{\text{Original Price}}$

That is: $\dfrac{\text{LOSS}}{\text{PAID}}$

The percentage loss is: $\dfrac{£40{,}000}{£185{,}000}$ = 0.216 or 21.6%

Consider this example:

EXAMPLE 19

Tony sold 16 Green Acre for £185,000 giving him a profit of 9%.
   How much did he originally buy the property?

The answer is this.

   The £185,000 includes the original price plus 9%.

   So, 100% + 9% = £185,000

   109% = £185,000

   $\dfrac{£185,000}{109\%}$ = £169,724.77

So, Tony originally paid £169,724.77 for the property.

Consider this example:

EXAMPLE 20

Tony sold 16 Green Acre for £185,000 giving him a loss of 14%.
   How much did he originally buy the property for?

The answer is this:

   The £185,000 includes the original price less 14%.

   So, 100% - 14% = £185,000

86% = £185,000

$$\frac{£185,000}{86\%} = £215,116.27$$

So, Tony originally paid £215,116.27 for the property and then sold it at a loss for £185,000.

Calculating Rental Yield:

There are two kinds of investors. There is the investor who is solely interested in capital appreciation when he invests. Our examples above cover this kind of investors.

However, there are other kinds of investors who are not too concerned about capital appreciation. They are more concerned about 'rental rate of return on investment'. This raises the good old 'appreciation versus yield' debate. There is no right or wrong approach. It is a question of preference.

So far, we have been looking at sales. What about where the investor is looking to rent out his property. How do you measure profitability?

Most investors measure the profitability of their investment by comparing how much they receive in rent to the interest if the money were placed in a savings account. You often hear them say, 'I want 6% return before I can buy that property…' Or they would say, 'If this property would guarantee a return of 8%, then I would consider it!'

Every investor is free to choose the acceptable rate of return he desires. But how do you calculate this?

The formula used by savvy investors is:

$$\frac{I}{R \times V}$$

This is known as the **IRV** formula. **I** means income. **R** means rate of return and **V** means price or value of the property

Step 1: In order to work out the **income** (**I**) or rent you want from a property, you simply multiply the **rate by value** (i.e. **R x V**).

Step 2: In order to work out the **rate of return** (**R**) you want from the property, you simply divide **income and value**. (i.e. **I/V**)

Step 3: In order to work out the **price** (**V**) you wish to pay for the property (i.e. how much a property is worth), you simply divide **income and rate** (i.e. **I/R**).

Consider this example

EXAMPLE 21

Tony wishes to buy 15 Okri Street, Manchester, which is a 2 bed terrace. The average rent for a 2 bed terrace on that street is £500 per month. Tony would only invest in that street if his investment could guarantee him 10% return per year. How much should Tony pay for 15 Okri Street?

The answer is this:

Apply the IRV formula.

Since the question is about how much the property is worth (i.e. 'price'), the appropriate formula is:

Price = **Income**
             Rates

$$P = \frac{I}{R}$$

$$P = \frac{£500 \text{ per month} \times 12}{10\%}$$

$$P = \frac{£6,000}{10\%}$$

P = £60,000.

Tony must offer no more than *£60,000* for 15 Okri Street.

Consider this example:

EXAMPLE 22

Tony wishes to buy 15 Okri Street, Manchester, which is a 2 bed terrace. The asking price is £95,000. The average rent for a 2 bed terrace on that street is £650 per month. Tony would only invest in this property if his investment could guarantee him 8% return per year. Does this property meet his requirement?

The answer is this:

Apply the IRV formula.

Since the question is about 'rate of return on investment', the appropriate formula is:

$$\text{Rate} = \frac{\text{Income}}{\text{Price}}$$

$$R = \frac{I}{V}$$

$$R = \frac{£650 \text{ per month} \times 12}{£95,000}$$

$$R = \frac{£7,800}{£95,000}$$

R = 0.082 or 8.2%

Since this property would likely generate a return of 8.2%, this would meet Tony's requirement.

Consider this example:

EXAMPLE 23

Tony has just purchased 15 Okri Street, Manchester, which is a 2 bed terrace. The price paid was £115,000. The street is known for generating rental return of 9% per year. How much rent should Tony ask his new tenant to pay?

The answer is this:

Apply the IRV formula.

Rent is treated as 'income'. Since the question is all about 'rental income', therefore the appropriate formula is: **income = rate x price**

I = R x V(price)

I = 9% x £115,000

I = £10,350 per year or £862.50 per month.

Tony should insert *£862.50* per month in the tenancy agreement.

Buying With (or Without) a Mortgage:

A time may come when an investor has to decide whether to buy a property outright (i.e. without a mortgage) or whether to take out a mortgage.

As an investor, you need to be able to use arithmetic to determine *whether or not* it would be profitable to take out a mortgage when purchasing a property.

An important indicator to help you determine whether the numbers stack up is the rate of 'Return on Investment' (ROI). The 'rate' of return on investment is the investor's net rental income expressed as a percentage of his initial deposit. In other words, the 'rate' of return converts the rental income into a percentage of the investor's down payment. So, if you invest £60,000 of your own money in a 'quantum property' and you then earn rent of £550 per month (or £6,600 per annum), your 'rate' of return would be 11%. This means that £6,600 is 11% of your initial investment (namely, £60,000). The higher the rate of return, the better since it means you are getting more for your money.

Consider this example:

EXAMPLE 24

Tony wishes to buy 15 Okri Street, Manchester, which is a 2 bed terrace. The asking price is £135,000. The average rent for a 2 bed terrace on that street is £550 per month. Should Tony buy the property outright with his money or should he take out a mortgage?

The answer is this: *The option which offers a better 'rate' of return on investment is the one Tony should adopt.*

First Option: Tony can use his money to purchase the property outright. This means Tony would have to put the whole £135,000 down.

His annual income would therefore be = £550 x 12 = £6,600. *But would this give him a good rate for his investment of £135,000?*

In order to work out his 'rate' of return, we need to apply the IRV formula:

Rate of ROI = $\frac{\text{Rental Income}}{\text{Purchase Price}}$ or $\frac{\text{Income}}{\text{Price}}$

Rate of **ROI** = $\frac{£6,600}{£135,000}$

Tony's 'rate' of **ROI** = 0.048 or 4.8%. This means his £135,000 investment only generate 4.8% income.

Second Option: The alternative option is for Tony to use 20% of his money (i.e. £27,000) as a deposit and he take out 80% mortgage (i.e. £108,000) for the balance.

If Tony takes out £108,000 mortgage at, say, 4%, his mortgage repayment may cost about £4,320 per year.

To find out Tony's actual profit, we need to deduct the mortgage payment (i.e. £4,320) from the net rental income (i.e. £6,600).

So Tony's net income = £6,600 - £4,320 = £2,280.

So investing £27,000 of his money will get Tony £2,280 net income per year.

In order to convert this into a 'rate' of return on investment, you need to applying the IRV formula, which is:

$$= \frac{\text{Net Rental Income}}{\text{Initial down payment}} \quad \text{or} \quad \frac{\text{Profit}}{\text{Investor's Money}}$$

Therefore, Tony's net **ROI** is: $\frac{£2,280}{£27,000}$

= 0.084 or 8.4%.

This means Tony's investment of £27,000 generates 8.4% income.

In view of the above, it is better for Tony to invest 20% of his money and take out a mortgage for the balance, since his **ROI** would be higher.

(v) Calculating Estate Agent's Commission:

If a seller uses an estate agent to secure the sale of his property, then that seller is responsible for the estate agent's commission.

The ***Estate Agents Act 1979*** provides that the estate agent must provide the seller with details of all fees to be charged in writing before agreeing to act. Apart from litigation, any complaint about, amongst others, fees can be raised with the Property Ombudsman, which covers 93% of sales agents.

Consider this example about commission:

EXAMPLE 25

A contract between Tony and Winman Estate Agent provides that the agent is entitled to 3.5% of sale price for 15 Okri Street, Manchester. Tony's solicitors managed to exchange contracts at a sale price of £415,000. How much will Winman Estate Agent earn from this sale?

The answer is this:

£415,000 x 3.5% = £14,525 commission.

The solicitors for Tony must deduct the sum of £14,525 from the proceeds of sale before transferring the balance (assuming there is no mortgage to redeem) to Tony, the seller.

(2) MATHS FOR HMO

HMO stands for House in Multiple Occupation. Pursuant to section 254 of the **Housing Act 2004**, HMO is a property rented out to at least 3 or more people (who are not from the same family), but share facilities such as kitchen and bathroom. So, a property with 3 bedsits where the tenants share a common kitchen and bathroom would be considered an HMO.

You must obtain a licence if your property is classified as an HMO by the relevant local authority. A licence is valid for 5 years. You can be fined up to £20,000 for renting out an unlicensed HMO.

Investors who invest in an HMO do so primarily because of the rental return this investment generates. It creates a multiple stream of passive income. *However, how would you know whether the HMO would be a profitable investment?*

The current and historical cash-flow amount generated by the HMO would determine whether you should invest in this property or not.

When working out the actual income the HMO can generate, the following 4 steps must be taken:

Step 1: Add up all the rents the HMO could generate per year on the basis that it was fully occupied. This is known as the Potential Gross Income (PGI).

Step 2: Then try and estimate what the expected loss of rent is likely to be as a result of tenant's turnover, occasional vacancies and non-payment of rents. This is called Vacancy and Collection Losses (VL)

Step 3: You should then deduct the amount arrived at as loss of rent (VL) from the potential gross income (PGI). The figure you arrive at is known as the Effective Gross Income (EGI).

Step 4: You then need to verify from the Seller the expenses associated with running the HMO. These expenses are known as Operating Expenses (OE). Examples of these are: council tax, building insurance, utility bills, maintenance, management fee, etc. These should be added up and deducted from the effective gross income (EGI). The figure you arrive at is known as the Net Operating Income (NOI). The NOI is effectively the actual income that gets to the hands of investor (assuming there is no mortgage to pay). The NOI is therefore the actual net income an investor may expect from the HMO.

The formula for calculating the NOI of an HMO is:

PGI - VL = EGI - OE = NOI

You can also change the format of the formula as follows:

```
    PGI
-   VL
   EGI
-   OE
   NOI
```

It is important to note that if you are taking out a mortgage to purchase an HMO, you must also deduct the yearly mortgage payment from the NOI to get to your net figure.

Consider this example:

EXAMPLE 26

Tony is thinking of buying 15 Okri Street, which is a building with 3 bedsits. Each bedsit is rented at £215 per month. The record shows that each tenant in the bedsit default at least 1 month of the year. The building insurance is £450 per year; estimated repair is about £500 per year and the letting agent charges a flat fee of £120 per month. The asking price is £85,000. What is the NOI of this HMO?

The answer is this:

Apply the formula:

```
             PGI
Minus    VL
             EGI
Minus    OE
             NOI
```

The result is:

```
   PGI (£215 x 3 bedsits x 12)        = £7,740
 - VL (£215 x 3 bedsits default)      =   £645
   EGI                                = £7,095
 - OE (insurance+repairs+agent fee)    £2,390
   NOI                                = £4,705
```

Thus, investing **£85,000** in this HMO (assuming there is no mortgage) would generate a yearly net operating income (**NOI**) of **£4,705**.

Consider this example:

EXAMPLE 27

Giving that the HMO at 15 Okri Street will generate a NOI of £4,705 per year, Tony would only invest in it if the NOI result in 7% return on investment or more. Does this HMO meet his requirement?

In order to calculate the rate of return, the **IRV** formula would have to now be applied. See example 22 above.

Since Tony is now more concerned about the 'rate', the formula is:

Rate = Income
   Price

Remember that the **NOI** is £4,705 and the property price is £85,000.

Therefore, R = £4,705
              £85,000

R = 0.0553 or 5.5%

This property would only generate 5.5% rate of return; since this falls short of the 7% Tony wants, he must walk away from this deal.

Consider this example:

EXAMPLE 28

Tony is thinking of buying 15 Okri Street, which is a building with 3 bedsits. Each bedsit is rented at £215 per month. The record shows that each tenant in the bedsit default at least 1 month of the year. The building insurance is £450 per year, estimated repair is about £500 per year and the letting agent charges a flat fee of £120 per month. The letting agent estimates that HMO of that size only generates about 6.5% return on investment. How much should Tony pay for the HMO?

The answer is this:

Apply the **IRV** formula.

Giving that the above scenario is about 'price', the formula is:

Price = Income
 Rates

You would see in example 26 above that the NOI is £4,705 and in example 28 the suggested rate of return is 6.5%.

So, P = £4,705
         6.5%

P = £72,384.62

Tony must offer no more than *£72,384.62* for the HMO.

(3) MATHS FOR OVERAGE

I dealt with 'overage' in chapter 7. You would recall that an 'overage' is a provision written into a contract of sale of land or property sold at undervalue. It describes the situation where a seller sells his land at a low value and then contracts to receive a percentage of the uplift when the land is eventually developed and sold by the buyer. In some circumstances, it is the seller who pays a percentage of the uplift to the buyer.

Both parties benefit from the overage arrangement in that the buyer acquires at a reduced price and the seller retains his right to share future profit as a result of improvement to the land.

The mathematical formula used to calculate '**overage**' is:

A - B x C%

A = the improved value of the land as a result of something done
B = the old (previous) value
C% = the percentage uplift agreed; the parties are free to agree whatever percentage during the negotiation

Consider this example.

EXAMPLE 29

S sells land to P for £23,000. The contract provides that, in the event of a sale by P, S shall be entitled to 40% of the proceeds of sale provided the sold price exceeds £70,000. P sells for £115,000. How much is S entitled to?

The answer is this:

Apply the formula: A - B x C%

£115,000 - £70,000 = £45,000 profit

£45,000 x 40% = £18,000 belongs to S

So, S is entitled to £18,000 and P can keep £27,000 (which represents 60%).

£18,000 + £27,000 = £45,000

(4) MATHS FOR NOVATION

I also covered the topic of 'novation' in chapter 7. You would recall that novation is an aspect of the Law of Contract, which allows a debt repayment obligation under a mortgage to be transferred from the previous borrower to another party in return for which the lender releases the previous borrower from the mortgage. The new party becomes the borrower under the same terms as the previous agreement.

One of the reasons why a borrower may wish to transfer the mortgage repayment obligation to third party may be because he wants to use the equity in the property as payment to settle a debt owed to that third party. Remember that the lender must agree to this before novation can succeed!

Consider this example.

EXAMPLE 30

Tony purchased 15 Okri street for £130,000 with 80% LVT from Broodhall Bank Plc. Tony owed Zak £39,000. Tony now wishes to transfer the property and the mortgage to Zak so that any equity in the property would be full satisfaction of his debt to Zak. Broodhall Bank

Plc has given its consent to the novation. Should Zak accept novation?

The answer is this:

£130,000 x 80% = £104,000 loan by Broodhall Bank Plc.

The equity in the property is £130,000 - £104,000(Bank loan) = £26,000

Tony only has £26,000 equity, which is insufficient to clear the £39,000 he owes Zak.

(5) MATHS FOR SHARED OWNERSHIP

Shared ownership, as a way of acquiring property, was covered in chapter 7. In a nutshell, shared ownership allows a purchaser to acquire a share of the title to a property whilst paying rent to the landlord for the unacquired share. For instance, a purchaser may acquire 40% of the title to a property and then pay rent to his landlord for the 60% share belonging to the landlord.

One advantage of shared ownership is that it allows people with smaller deposit, who are struggling to raise a mortgage, acquire property even in areas with high property prices, such as London.

However, when considering shared ownership, you should arithmetically assess whether it is cheaper to rent or to acquire using the shared ownership scheme.

Consider this example.

EXAMPLE 31

Walesbridge Association is offering a 2 bed shared ownership flat as a resale for the price of £150,000, for a 60% share. The full market value is £250,000. The full rent for a 2 bed flat valued at £250,000 in the area is £1,300 per month. Tony has a savings of £8,000. Should Tony pay the full rent for the property or should he acquire the 60% share and just pay rent on the 40% share?

The answer is this:

(a) PURCHASE PRICE: £150,000 (a 60% share of the full market price of £250,000)
(b) DEPOSIT: £8,000
(c) MORTGAGE: £150,000 - £8,000 deposit = £142,000
(d) MONTHLY MORTGAGE PAYMENT: £695 per month on the balance of £142,000
(e) RENT: £450 per month on the 40% share belonging to Walesbridge Association.
(f) TOTAL MONTHLY EXPENDITURE: £695 + £450 = £1,145 per month.

From the above calculation, you can see that it makes investment sense for Tony to acquire a 60% share of the property and pay rent on the 40% share rather than pay full rent of £1,300. By taking the decision to acquire the shared ownership property, he has saved £155 per month.

CHAPTER 10: THE MATHEMATICS OF STAMP DUTY

'He that would have the fruit must climb the tree' – Thomas Fuller, 1608-1661

The Stamp Duty Land Tax (SDLT) is a tax payable to HMRC by a purchaser buying property in England and Wales above £125,000.

A new rate of SDLT was introduced on the 4th December 2014, which applies to various properties. The table below shows the new rates:

Minimum Property Purchase Price	Maximum Purchase Price	Stamp Duty Rates
£0	£125,000	0%
£125,001	£250,000	2%
£250,001	£925,000	5%
£925,001	£1.5 million	10%
Over £1.5 million	Above	12%

If you purchase a property for £125,000 or below, Stamp duty is not payable. If you buy a property for £185,000, you would not pay stamp duty for the first £125,000. You would however pay stamp duty at the rate of 2% for the difference between £125,001 and £185,000 (which is roughly £60,000). So £60,000 x 2% = £1,200 payable as tax.

If you go to www.gov.uk/stamp-duty-land-tax-calculators, you can use the SDLT calculators to work out your tax. However, you cannot use this calculator for residential properties with chargeable consideration above £500,000. You would need to perform the calculation manually.

Consider this example.

EXAMPLE 32

Tony purchased 15 Okri street, London WC2 for £670,000. How much stamp duty is payable?

The answer is this:

(1) **Step 1**: £0 - £125,000 = no stamp duty
(2) **Step 2**: £125,001 - £250,000 = £125,000 x 2% = £2,500
(3) **Step 3**: £250,001 - £670,000 = £419,999 x 5% = £20,999.95
(4) **Step 4**: Add £2,500 + £20,999.95 = £23,499.95 (round up to £23,500) payable as stamp duty.

So, Tony must pay £23,500 to HMRC as stamp duty.

CHAPTER 11: THE ECONOMICS OF PROPERTY INVESTMENTS

'Everything factual is already a theory' – Johann Wolfgang von Goethe

House ownership and property prices are topical issues today. Home ownership has long been one of the bedrock of investor's wealth in the UK. Over the last 10 years, the value of UK housing has rocketed by about £1.4 trillion to stand at about £5.75 trillion. The price of a starter home has increased by 48 times since 1969. According to the Office for National Statistics, the average price in 2002 was £134,373 but by 2012 the average price rose to £230,358.

What drives prices?

In a free market economy, the principles of 'demand' and 'supply' affect the housing market just like any other market. Although house prices vary from area to area, demand and supply nevertheless determines price.

DEMAND

Residential properties are acquired for a number of reasons: for owner-occupation; as a second home; for holiday let or for buy-to-let. Today, almost 2 million private landlords own 4.9 million properties. As opposed to owner-occupation, the buy-to-let market is one of the fastest growing and takes a big chunk of the UK housing stock.

In economic terms, the higher the demand for property the higher the price of property. As demand for property increases, it forces the price of properties upward. This is illustrated in the graph below:

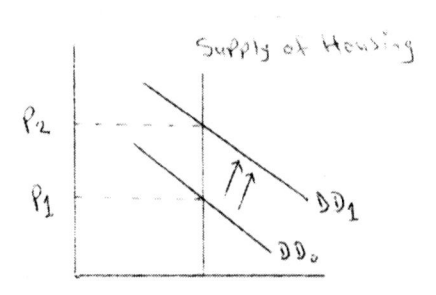

There are numerous factors affecting the demand for housing. They are:

(1) Income/wages
(2) Availability of loans/mortgages
(3) Government policies
(4) Employment
(5) Social attitudes
(6) Sensationalism
(7) Speculation
(8) Population trends
(9) The rental market trends

(1) Income

The income a person earns affects whether he can afford to buy a property. The higher your income the more likely you can get on the property ladder.

(2) Availability of loans/mortgages

The availability of mortgages affects property prices. The demand for property would increase if people have easier access to credit. The Council of Mortgage Lenders said that between 2013 and 2014, buy-to-let lending increased by 28%. In 2013, more than £20 billion was lent to landlords. Lenders are showing an appetite to lend. According to Paragon, there are now more than 700 buy-to-let mortgage deals available to investors. This effectively pushes up prices as more buyers enter the property market.

(3) Government Policies

Governments have numerous methods they use to encourage or discourage demand for properties. In a sluggish economy (or where first-time buyers cannot get on the property ladder), the government can increase demand for property by doing the following:

(i) Reduce stamp duty or raise the threshold
(ii) Reduce interest rate through the Bank of England
(iii) Promote the Help to Buy scheme
(iv) Promote the Help to Buy ISA
(v) By quantitative easing, etc.

(4) Employment

The more people in remunerative work, the more they will be willing and able to commit to a mortgage to buy property. The fall in unemployment rates creates a high consumer confidence, which feeds into spending.

(5) Social Attitudes

The British have a long and consistent love affair with bricks and mortar. You only have to attend social functions and eavesdrop into conversations! Thus, a country with a high desire to buy property is more likely to have high demands for housing than countries with low desires (such as Germany).

(6) Sensationalism

The idea of buying properties are being planted into people's consciousness through popular TV programmes such as 'Homes Under the Hammer'; 'A Place in the Sun'; 'Location, Location, Location'; 'Escape to the Country', etc.

This creates a desire in people to be an overnight success in property investments.

(7) Speculation

It is no secret that house prices have increased since the last 10 years. For this reason, people tend to invest in property in the belief that prices would carry on rising. This speculative attitude leads to an increase in demand for housing.

(8) Population trends

Increase in the population can influence demand for property, because as population increases, demand for places to live also increases. Population may increase because we live longer, or because of immigration, or because of the birth rates, etc.

The data from the Office for National Statistics shows that as at 2011, the population of England and Wales stood at 56.1 million, a rise of 3.7 million since 2001. In the same period, the number of foreign-born residents increased from 4.6 million to 7.5 million. The population in London is set to reach a record of 8.6 million people. As at June 2014, the UK population stood at 64.6 million. This has led to housing shortage with increase in the number of buyers.

Another effect of a growing population is the impact it has on social housing. There are almost 1.4 million households on social housing waiting lists. However, with council houses being lost to tenants buying their council flats, this waiting list is likely to grow thereby putting more pressure on the housing stock.

(9) The Rental Market trends

The rental market trends can, and do, influence demand for property.
In a free market economy, if the demand for a product increases, suppliers tend to ensure more of that product is available to capture the increasing demand. The same is true in the housing market. As rent soars because of demand, investors buy more properties to rent out so as to increase their yield.

The English Housing Survey found that in 2013-14, 19% (i.e. 4.4 million) of households in England were renting privately. In the same period, BTL investment increased to capture the rental market. The survey concluded that the Private Rental Sector (PRS) had doubled in size since 2002. As at April 2015, there were about 5 million rented accommodations in the UK.

SUPPLY

The supply of housing also affects price. The supply of property refers to the availability of property for sale or rent. In economic terms, the supply of property is ***inelastic*** because it reacts slowly to the fluctuation of prices. This is because the supply of new homes by construction cannot react as quickly when there is an increase in demand. The ***Housing Federation*** said that although Britain needs 245,000 new homes per year, only 125,000 a year are being built. In March 2015, the ***Organisation for Economic Cooperation & Development* (OECD)** warned that the supply of new housing in the UK is failing to meet demand.

There are a number of factors affecting the supply of housing. They are as follows:

(1) Planning policy
(2) Availability of land to build
(3) Social housing
(4) Price of the factors of production
(5) Price generally

(1) Planning policy: The ability to build homes will depend on how easy it is to get planning permission for construction. In England, the process of obtaining planning permission is slow and involves neighbours objecting to the application, which tends to jeopardize property construction. If planning permission is refused, the developer would not be able to supply the property, since he is prevented from building it.

(2) Availability of land to build: The availability of land also affects supply of housing. The UK is an island. Land is finite. If there is no land to build, there can be no supply of housing.

Some parts of the UK are designated as 'greenbelts' and 'brownfield sites'. These sites are difficult to build on as planners are reluctant to encourage urban sprawl.

(3) Social housing: The willingness of the government to build housing would affect the total supply of housing. However, local authorities have stopped building. Even council flats are being sold off under the right to buy scheme. The housing stock in the public sector is therefore dwindling. In fact, in 2014 Enfield Council broke with tradition and went ahead to form a company with a view to buying properties. In 2015, Westminster Council began to purchase properties outside London.

(4) Price of the factors of production: The supply of housing may be affected by wage rises, rising cost of land or building material increases.

(5) Price generally: A rise in the price of houses may encourage sellers to put their property on the market to benefit from capital appreciation.

Author's Remark

A friend of mine who was an estate agent was trying to persuade me to invest in Goldthorpe, near Doncaster. He told me that because of a shortage of local authority housing, the council was contacting local landlords with vacant properties to let them to council tenants, who are on the council's waiting list. This show there is always going to be demand for housing!

APPENDICES

APPENDIX i: THE PARETO PRINCIPLE

Faber est quisque fortunae suae (every man is architect of his own fortune)

The Pareto Principle was developed by Joseph M Juran. It was named after an Italian economist called Vilfredo Pareto.

The Pareto Principle simply avers that, for many events, 80% of the outcome comes from 20% of a source. Mathematically, this became known as the 80/20 rule.

This rule is now commonly used in business. Some business organisations have identified that 80% of their sales comes from 20% of their customers. The value of this principle is to remind us to focus on 20% of the thing that matters.

In property investment, concentrate on the investment, which generates the most returns. If there are 20% of your investments, which generate 80% of your profit, then that is where you need to focus. Your 'energy' of profit would be increased if you increase that aspect of the investment by increasing it beyond 20%.

APPENDIX ii: HOW TO FIND PROPERTY BARGAINS
'Finder keeper' - Unknown

It is every investor's dream to acquire bargain properties. These are properties bought below market value. In order to successfully apply the 'property quantum formula', you need to be able to find bargain properties. There is plenty of help available online. You just need to know where to search. Some of the helpful websites to go to are as follows:

Wreckoftheweek.co.uk:
This blog regularly publishes various properties in the UK, which need substantial amounts of work done. It offers property search services and tips for purchasing these type of properties.

Unmodernised.com:
This website lists properties which need renovation or redevelopment with or without planning permission.

Uniquepropertybulletin.org:
This is an online weekly newsletter about various types of properties in the UK ranging from £10,000 to £10,000,000.

Whitehotproperty.co.uk:
This is another website with a large database of properties, which includes new homes, repossessed and probate properties.

Zoopla.co.uk or rightmove.co.uk:
These two websites are two of the most used. You can search using post codes, areas or cities. You can view all kinds of properties, residential and commercial.

www.hbosplc.com:
This is another useful website. On this website you can find useful historical data about the movement of prices in the housing market.

PropertyAuctionAction.co.uk:
This free site lists all the major UK residential and commercial property auctions and forthcoming property auctions with easily navigated links to the property auction catalogue. It is really easy to follow.

There are other individual auction websites such as Allsop, Barnard Marcus, Savills, Harman Healy, Pugh, Edward Mellor, etc.

APPENDIX iii: STEP-BY-STEP PROPERTY TRANSACTION GUIDE

'Qui audet adipiscitur (he who dares wins)'

This guide provides an overview of the process to follow when investing in property.

STEP 1: When investing in property, the first step to take is to ascertain where (i.e. which location) you wish to invest in. The important indicators to look out for have already been covered in chapter 4. Ensure you research the area.

Your reasons for investing would determine the location to invest in. If you want a rapid (or quick) capital appreciation of your investment, then certain areas would not be suitable. Investors talk about the North/South divide in the British property market. However, if all you want is a reasonable yield from housing benefit tenants, then location may not be such a big issue if you are buying low-priced properties.

The checklist below may be useful to adopt:

- Have you identified why you wish to invest in the area?
- Have you conducted sufficient research of the area?
- Is there evidence of economic growth in the area?
- Is there employment in the area?
- Are there good transport links to the area?
- Are there good social and entertainment facilities in the area?
- Is this a good location to invest in?
- Are rents rising in the area?
- Are prices rising in the area?

STEP 2: When you identify the location, you then need to work out how much you are looking to spend on a property in that area. Make sure you prepare a budget of your income and expenditure.

Once you have worked out how much you need for the investment, next thing is to take steps to raise the funds. You may visit your mortgage broker with a view to obtaining a mortgage from a lender. Alternatively, you may have cash saved. I identified various sources of funds in chapter 7. You may use that as your checklist. What ever your source of fund is, it is essential that you have your fund in place at this stage.

STEP 3: After you have sorted out your funds, you can then start sourcing properties to buy. You can source properties by:
(i.) Visiting local agents in the area;
(ii) Checking online (e.g. Rightmove or Zoopla, etc). Promap at www.promap.co.uk allows you access to all the ordinance survey's maps and aerial photography of the UK together with points of interests and street level of an area;
(iii) Attending auctions; and
(iv) Driving through the area and knocking on doors; look out for 'for sale' signs; speak to family and friends to find out if they know of anyone selling; put up notices on corner-shops informing sellers that you can buy their properties etc.

STEP 4: Once you have identified the property, you can then arrange to view the property. Make sure you take pictures of the inside of the property to remind yourself of the state of the property.

The checklist below may be useful to adopt:

- Find out from the seller whether the property is freehold or leasehold;
- If leasehold, find out about the ground rent, service charge and terms of the lease. Further, find out about the identity of the landlord or whether there is an 'absent landlord'. Note: some lenders will not lend if the landlord cannot be found;
- Find out from the seller whether the area is under a Selective Licensing Scheme. Some local authorities select a rundown area and make it compulsory for landlords to obtain a licence before they can rent out their property. Licence would only be given where the property is in good habitable condition;
- Find out whether the property is listed. A building with architectural or historical interests can be classified as listed. This means you cannot extend, alter or demolish it without a special permission from the local planning authority;
- Take note whether the property needs renovation/repairs;
- Can you negotiate a price reduction because of the repairs required?
- Check to ensure the property does not suffer from subsidence. Subsidence occurs if there is a movement or shift of the earth surface causing damage to properties; and
- Check with the neighbours to ensure there is no boundary dispute.

STEP 5: If you like the property, you can then put in an offer. Most agents or auctioneers would ask you for your proof of funds and proof of address in order to comply with the money laundering rules.

STEP 6: If your offer is accepted, it is advisable to instruct a surveyor to inspect the property with a view to ascertaining whether there are any foundational or environmental problems. You must also instruct a firm of solicitors to investigate title and carry out the conveyancing work.

STEP 7: After all the due diligence, you must transfer funds for the purchase to your solicitors. The amount you transfer would include the purchase price, solicitors' fees, disbursements, stamp duty fee (if applicable) and land registration fees. If you are using a mortgage, your solicitor would ask the lender to transfer the loan amount to his law firm's client account, which is to be used for your transaction.

STEP 8: Your solicitors would contact you to sign the contract. Contracts could then be exchanged. At this stage, there is a binding contract. The seller and buyer are bound to complete the transaction. A date is fixed in the contract for completion. At this point, the buyer must put in place building insurance.

STEP 9: On the completion day, your solicitor would transfer the purchase price to the vendor's solicitors and ownership (or title) transfers to the buyer, who now becomes the new owner. Your solicitor would pay the stamp duty, if applicable, from the money you transferred to him. The solicitors would also register your ownership with the Land Registry under the Land Registration Act 1925.

STEP 10: If the property needs to be renovated, you can at this stage contact your builders for a renovation quote. Decide whether you would be using a project manager. If not, then at least ensure that: (a) you go through the surveyor's report with your builders; (b) prepare a contract for your builders to sign; and (c) agree a payment structure with them. Lastly, when the renovation is completed, ensure that you go through the Schedule of Work with your builders to ascertain that they have fully carried out what was agreed. Remember that by renovating or repairing your property, you are adding value to it. I referred to this as 'value engineering' in chapter 2.

STEP 11: When the property is ready for occupation, you may instruct a local letting agent to let and manage the property on your behalf.

If you decide to instruct a letting agent, it is important to be aware that since 27 May 2015, the ***Consumer Rights Act, 2015*** provides that Letting Agents and property management businesses must display their fees and charges to clients. The fees and charges must be displayed in a conspicuous place where the agent meet clients or potential client or on their website.

The displayed fees must include (a) an adequate description of each fee and its purpose; (b) whether the fee is payable for the accommodation or by each tenant; (c) the total amount of the fee inclusive of VAT; (d) the method of calculating the fee.

In England only, the letting agent must also display a statement as to whether the business is a member of a client money protection scheme and a statement that they are a member of a redress scheme and the name of that scheme, if applicable.

A penalty of up to £5,000 can be imposed by trading standards services for breaches of these requirements.

However, if you decide to manage the property yourself, then the checklist below may be useful to adopt:

- You must familiarise yourself with landlord and tenant laws;
- You must have basic knowledge of tenant's rights;
- You must have basic knowledge of landlord's obligations;

- You must have basic knowledge of the Deposit Protection Scheme (DPS);
- Check to ensure you can get a reference for the potential tenant;
- Ensure you know how to look for, and vet, the tenant;
- Ensure that you carry out a risk assessment for Legionnaires Disease
- Ensure you take a reading of the gas and electric meters
- Ensure you know how to serve the necessary notice for termination of the tenancy (e.g. Section 8 Notice or Section 21 Notice).
- Ensure you obtain landlord insurance to cover damage to your property, accidents and/or loss of rent.

STEP 12: Instead of renting out your 'quantum property', you may decide to sell it immediately after renovation. If this is your preferred option, then you have to consider whether to sell at an auction or through an estate agent.

If you choose to go down the auction route, there are many websites that list most residential auctioneers and their auction dates. A useful website is *PropertyAuctionAction.co.uk*: this free site lists all the major UK residential and commercial property auctions and forthcoming property auctions with easily navigated links to the property auction catalogue. It is really easy to follow.

Once you have contacted your chosen property auctioneer, you would be required to send to the property auctioneer the following:
- a signed copy of the terms and conditions of the auction
- proof of property ownership (e.g copy of the land register)
- proof of ID (e.g. copy passport and utility bill in your name)
- EPC
- gas safety certificate

- details of your solicitor
- land registry and local authority search results (yours solicitor would supply this to them)
- payment for putting your property in the auction catalogue. The auctioneer would tell you the amount to pay.

Auction property sales usually legally complete in 28 days unless you specify that you want a shorter period of completion. This has to be inserted as a 'special condition' in the sale contract. If the 'quantum property' is sold at the auction, the proceeds of sale is transferred to your solicitor, who would deduct his fee and the auctioneer's fee before sending any balance to you (assuming there is no mortgage to redeem).

Alternatively, if you choose to sell your property through an estate agent, then it is prudent to use an agent at the locality where the property is. This is because the agent understands the local market and the prevailing property prices. You can find a local agent online, by recommendations or by consulting the local paper.

Once you have contacted the estate agent, the agent would require you to sign their terms and conditions. He will then visit the property to take photos and measurement for advertisement purposes. You would then be required to send him the following:

- proof of property ownership (e.g copy of the land register)
- proof of ID (eg copy passport and utility bill in your name)
- EPC
- gas safety certificate
- details of your solicitor

After your property has been advertised and a buyer is found, the agent would prepare the Memorandum of Sale, which contains the details of the buyer and seller, the address and price of the property, and the solicitors' details. This document would then be sent to the buyer and seller's solicitors, who would then carry out the conveyancing work.

POSTSCRIPT: UNENCUMBERED PROPERTY: A BETTER DERIVATIVE

'It always seem impossible until it is done' – Nelson Mandela

My aim in this book has been to show to my readers a different way of thinking when it comes to property investment.

Whilst you might have your way of approaching investments, there is no harm in understanding other ways. *Audite et alteram partem,* (listen even to the other side).

In this book, I expounded the 'Property Quantum Formula' as another way of approaching property investment.

It is no secret that I have never been in favour of financial product investments. They are too complicated to monitor, too risky to put my money in and too artificial to behold.

The so-called financial experts have long lied to us about the security of 'securities'. The 2008 global financial meltdown is a stark reminder that things can, and do, go wrong.

In the good old days, when a person borrowed money from the bank, the debt remained with that bank.

Today, the experts have engineered and manufactured complicated financial products. The 'financial innovations' are such that debts are packaged and sold on. These debts are pooled and called Asset-Backed Securities (**ABS**), which can be turned into Collateralised Debt Obligations (**CDO**). Risks are then shifted from one party to the other.

Another interesting financial instrument is 'derivatives'. Investment banks play a key role in promoting and trading these products.

Derivatives are financial instruments that are like a bet, but operate as an insurance policy. They purport to hedge against risks. However, if another global economic downturn should recur, derivatives would clearly fail as a 'vaccination against recession': if **Bank Y** should sell insurance to **Bank Z**, but **Bank Y** then goes into financial difficulty, **Bank Z** would not be well protected!

Although the Financial Conduct Authority (FCA) regulates the financial services industry, there is no requirement that all Over-The-Counter (OTC) derivatives should go through regulated clearing houses. There is also no total guarantee that the Central Counterparty (CCP) can cover all possible losses or do so indefinitely. This creates an exposure!

If you are worried about rising interest rates or unemployment or a sluggish economy, the main asset that would pay out if your fears are realised is 'unencumbered property'. Properties free of mortgages are unencumbered properties. Managed well, the gains from this property-derivative should offset any losses from underlying price movements or economic problems.

The rental payments are made irrespective of the movement of prices. If there is a default, the investor can very quickly change the payer or the source from private paying to public paying (i.e. Housing Benefit).

Quod Erat Demonstrandum (QED)